Graceful Endings

Navigating the Journey of Loss and Grief

Linda Kavelin-Popov

Author of *A Pace of Grace*

Graceful Endings: Navigating the Journey of Loss and Grief
by Linda Kavelin-Popov

Publisher: Virtues Project International www.virtuesproject.com
Create Space, www.amazon.com

Cover Art: Jalal'iyyih Quinn www.jalaliyyihquinn.com
Cover and book design: Dan Popov

LIBRARY OF CONGRESS CATALOGING-IN-PUBLICATION DATA

Popov, Linda Kavelin; Kavelin-Popov, Linda; Graceful Endings;
virtues; The Virtues Project; end of life, grief, loss, companioning,
death, dying, hospice, palliative care.

ISBN 13:978-1479165315   10:147916531X

Published in the United States

Other books by Linda Kavelin-Popov

The Family Virtues Guide

Sacred Moments: Daily Meditations on the Virtues

The Virtues Project Educator's Guide: Simple Ways to Create a
Culture of Character

A Pace of Grace: the Virtues of a Sustainable Life

DEDICATION

To my beloved brother, John, who stepped into the journey of death as a pilgrim exploring a grand mystery.

John is my younger brother, and a lifelong soul friend. He has also been a cherished colleague to me and my husband Dan, since the three of us founded The Virtues Project in 1990. In 1988, John took a break from his work with Walt Disney Imagineering to visit us in British Columbia. Over brunch at the Empress Hotel in Victoria, he expressed a desire "to be of more direct service to humanity." That defining moment led to our collaboration on a global initiative that has spread to more than ninety-eight countries.

John resigned from Disney, and the three of us spent what we called our "summer of discernment" in a small rented waterside cottage near Victoria, on Vancouver Island, off the west coast of Canada. We reflected on how we could do something to counteract violence by children against themselves and each other. As a psychotherapist working with suicidal and violent youth, I had discovered that at the core, violence is a failure of hope, the disease of meaninglessness. Understanding the meaning of their lives would be a healing step. So, we looked for the meaning of life in the sources Dan had studied for years – the sacred texts of the world's religions. We found that at the core, like a silver thread of unity running through them all, are virtues – the purpose and meaning of life, the link between humanity and the Divine.

We bought a two-bedroom home on Salt Spring Island, with a large out-building where we produced our first book, The Family Virtues Guide. To our amazement, this home-grown initiative started a global movement. Within two months, our "self-published" (i.e. photocopied) book, then in a 3-hole binder spread to over twenty countries, by word of mouth alone. It has since been published by Penguin and has been translated into more than a dozen languages.

After a few years, Dan and I were traveling the world speaking and teaching, and John went back to work with Disney. He had designed Mr. Toad's Wild Ride at Disneyland and returned to over-see Asia for Animal Kingdom in Orlando. Finally he was assigned to Japan for six years as Design Director for Tokyo Disneyland. In 2006, he came home to our island, bought a beautiful three-story log house ten minutes away from us, and decided to devote his retirement years to The Virtues Project. I was thrilled to have him back. Our phone bills had been astronomical.

When we learned that John was going to die, it stirred an intimation that had lingered in the back of my mind for years, a knowing that I would care for him in his last days. Dan and I chose to stop our world travels and remain with John for the duration.

After John's second and last brain surgery, Dan had the grace to realize that we needed to move in with him. I was run ragged driving between our home and John's. Dan and I remained with John until his death seven months later. For my privacy-loving, self-described recluse husband, this was a true sacrifice, and I can never thank him enough.

I was inspired to write *Graceful Endings* first and foremost to share John's remarkable attitude toward death. I am also moved to describe my parallel experience of grief, and what allowed me to survive it, learn to accept it, and eventually value it. Losing my longest life companion left a vast hole in my being, but it has also opened doors.

Finally, I believe that John's exquisite quality of life throughout his illness prevailed in part because we immersed ourselves in the Five Strategies of The Virtues Project and in the virtues themselves. They provided a frame of reference, or, to be more accurate, a frame of Reverence for this end of life passage.

It is inevitable that we will all encounter loss and death. My hope is that *Graceful Endings* will be a helpful companion, enabling you not only to cope with grief, but to discern the gifts on your own journey.

Linda Kavelin-Popov
Salt Spring Island, British Columbia

I THE JOURNEY OF GRIEF

"There is a crack in everything. That's how the light gets in."
Leonard Cohen, lyrics of *Anthem*

Grief begins at the moment a sudden death occurs or a life-changing diagnosis is received, and it endures long after the death of a loved one. It is a shape-shifter that moves into our lives, taking unexpected forms and coming in unpredictable patterns.

It has many faces. We can accept its presence or we can resist, but there are consequences to both. It may at times feel like a hideous nightmare we wish only to escape, but I have found that the best way through it is to befriend it.

Viewing grief and loss as a journey of initiation, we are no longer victims, but navigators. We can then move beyond mere survival to receive its surprising gifts. When tended with love and compassion, grief is a portal leading to a deeper experience of Grace – the sense that everything comes to us from a source of love, to bring us joy or to make us grow.

1 THE JOURNEY BEGINS

"We must embrace pain and burn it as fuel for our journey."
Kenji Miyazawa, poet and author

I thought I was an expert on grief until the day we learned that my brother John had incurable brain cancer. Not until I was losing one of my closest loves did I have an inkling of its dimensions. Having worked as a hospice spiritual care director and a psychotherapist for decades, I had companioned many dying individuals and their family members. But witnessing grief and being the one in grief are a world apart. Nothing prepared me for the unexpected loss of my younger brother – so radiant, so healthy – my first friend.

There is a saying that life is what happens when we're making other plans. When someone we love is diagnosed with a terminal illness, life suddenly contracts into a small space with that person at the center. We circle the wagons. We weave a cocoon. We become fiercely protective. Everything else seems to fall away. We are enveloped in single-pointed concentration on their wellbeing. Time is rapidly absorbed in medical appointments, changes to our schedule, changes to our lives. And then there is the grief. It comes unbidden, often so suddenly that it takes our breath away.

Getting the News
I sat with John as the radiation oncologist explained to him the confirmed diagnosis of Glio Blastoma Multiform brain cancer, with the dire prognosis that he would live only a few months, even with radiation and chemotherapy. Without it, the time he had left would be even shorter.

As we left the cancer clinic, John was quiet. He looked stunned. "What do you need now?" I asked, holding my own tears in check. "Breakfast!!" he bellowed, and we both laughed. He had been advised by friends to go on a restrictive anti-cancer alkaline diet, giving up coffee, sugar, and other things he loved ever since our family doctor had said it looked like cancer. Now that the diagnosis was confirmed, his only desire was for comfort.

As he chowed down on bacon, eggs and pancakes, slurping coffee with great gusto, I said, "The condemned man ate a hearty breakfast." His laughter erupted loudly and he sprayed coffee all over his fried potatoes. Humor can be a healing balm in this surreal experience of death and loss.

The way grief manifests itself is unique to each of us. The way it shifts and changes differs from person to person. It is mercilessly unpredictable in its force and form. John spent the days following his diagnosis in a state of shock and seemed quietly puzzled – a common first response both for those who learn that they are dying and those who love them.

My immediate experience was vastly different. A tsunami of sorrow blind-sided and engulfed me. I was drowning. The devastating possibility that John's life would be shortened rose up and swallowed me for hours at a time. It intensified without warning, leaving me utterly spent, bereft. It felt as if my core had imploded and was suddenly missing, not questioning God's existence or presence, but my own. It put me in mind of the movie, "Death Becomes Her", where Meryl Streep and Goldie Hawn, as living ghosts, shoot huge holes in each other's torsos.

Have Compassion for Yourself
We live in a culture which teaches us not to whine or complain, to accentuate the positive, to have a fighting spirit. Above all, God forbid we should ever indulge in self-pity. It is not surprising that in the midst of intense emotions, along comes guilt to assault us, compounding our natural sadness. I caught myself feeling terribly ashamed of my intense grief – a reaction I had witnessed often in people close to the dying. My inner judge kept fussing, "Get a hold of yourself! Where is your faith?" Above all, I longed to be sufficiently detached so that I could be present to John and give him space for his own feelings.

One day in my daily reflection time, I said aloud, "For heaven's sake, Linda, have some compassion for yourself!" Compassion was a balm to my soul that day. A sweet tranquillity suffused me, brought my shoulders down from around my ears, and allowed me to relax into a much needed state of meditation. A clear, powerful message came to mind, one which I could not fully grasp in that moment but which sustained me – and John as well – as the roller-coaster ride of dealing with emotional, medical and end of life realities progressed: "Seek a vibrant relationship with the unknown." In retrospect, this guidance reminds me of dancing, learning to ski, or riding a horse. One has to surrender, move with the rhythm as it changes, and stay light in the saddle, not fearfully resisting every shift but leaning into it.

By whatever means, it is essential to tap deeply into compassion for ourselves as soon as we can. See a counsellor, begin a grief journal, join a grief group, or talk with an intimate friend who will serve as your story-keeper throughout the journey. A caring person who is willing to hear the details as they unfold is an invaluable gift. I called on every one of these tools.

Build a Support System
When we are facing the death of a loved one, one of our first tasks is to ask ourselves, "What do I need, to get through this and to be the companion I want to be to my loved one?" The road ahead, whatever time is involved, is unknown and frightening. To my surprise, I found that although there was an army of people and resources directed toward John, I had to scramble for help myself. It is essential for primary caregivers to create our own circle of support in order to give the best we have to the dying.

Accepting our need for help is the first step in discerning who can provide it and where we can go for it. We need people willing to companion us, whether a hospice volunteer or a professional grief counselor, a friend, or a family member. Here is what we need from them:
  They have empathy for our pain. They understand that

sometimes the baptism of our tears is the most healing balm. They don't rush us past the tears or push us into hope. Sometimes they cry with us.

They don't shy away from asking questions for fear of the answers. They have compassionate curiosity, which is an expression of genuine presence. They ask, "How is this for you?" and "What's your biggest worry?" Their loving silence allows us to empty our cups whether we're sad, mad, scared, or numb.

They know we need humor too. The healthiest way to deal with grief is to go into it deeply, and then get our attention off it entirely, doing something fun or just laughing with a friend.

They (mostly) avoid pithy or religious sayings that can invalidate feelings if said at the wrong time – in the middle of an expression of sadness, for example. Yet, sometimes the right words ignite hope. My husband said, "We plan for the best and cope with the rest." – often repeated and strangely comforting. After allowing me to finish crying, a friend quoted Julian of Norwich: "Remember, this too shall pass. All will be well." It's all in the timing.

They offer simple, helpful services like taking out the garbage if we're tied up with hospital visits. They bring food, which at times we just don't have the energy or attention to prepare. They offer to drive.

When we surround ourselves with care, we are able to encircle our loved ones with grace, giving them our full, compassionate presence.

"I don't need a certain number of friends,
just a number of friends I can be certain of."
Alice Walker, author

SUSTAINING VIRTUES:

Compassion is deep empathy for the suffering of others. Compassion flows freely from the heart when we let go of judgments and seek to understand. In facing death, we need to direct that compassion toward ourselves as well.

Humility is openness to the lessons of life. We don't expect to do it all ourselves. We are willing to receive help as well as to give it.

HEALING STEPS:

1. Have compassion for yourself as well as your loved one. Become a good listener and find good listeners.

2. Consider starting a grief journal. It can be a helpful companion.

3. Reach out for help.

The Fire of Anger

Grief sometimes erupts as thin-skinned, hyper-reactive anger. We sometimes feel so helpless and out of control that all we can do is ride the choppy seas of irritability and crankiness until we come to calmer waters. For many men, socialized to repress sadness and terrorized out of tears at a young age, anger is often the only way they know to express loss. Sometimes, the anger becomes internalized as depression edged with guilt. "Why couldn't I have been a better husband when I had the chance?" "Why couldn't I save her?"

Here is an example. A family gathered in an emergency room waiting area as doctors worked feverishly over the lifeless body of the youngest child. Their car had been side-swiped by a drunk driver. When the doctor shook his head and told them that the five year old had died, her fifteen year old brother sat stunned in silence, her mother wept bitterly, and her father began railing loudly against the driver. Men of western culture rarely have access to the expression of pure grief.

For a while after John died, I felt irrationally angry at everyone else in my life for not being John. In the months just after his death, I found the "silent treatment" from others intolerable. I felt absurdly furious if I encountered a friend or even an acquaintance who said nothing, as if nothing had happened, when in truth, my world as I knew it had ended. I knew intellectually that they simply did not know what to say, yet the pain arose of its own accord. One unfortunate and innocent woman I was having dinner with said that she believed we bring illness on ourselves, and was expressing her guilt at her own lingering illness. I suddenly erupted, "Do you honestly believe John caused his brain cancer?" Her brown face paled and I immediately apologized. My personal boundaries were terribly frayed in those days, as if there were a volcano in my brain that exploded without my permission.

Bereavement

Bereavement is the experience of grief after a death. The world is off kilter and we often feel like a ship that has lost its moorings. John's twin brother Tommy said, "John was my anchor. Now I'm adrift." Tommy and I both experienced a sense of outrage that John's bright light had gone from our lives. To whom does one direct this vague, diffuse anger?

My friend, Jane, described her grief at losing not only her elderly father to death, but in another way, her aging mother who went into a tailspin of irritability for weeks after her husband had passed. Jane said that she simply "couldn't land." She would start to read, only to put the book down, would turn on a favorite radio program and quickly turn it off, start to do something and suddenly lose interest. This disorienting experience continued until her mother emerged from the cranky woods and was more herself.

The waves of grief continue for months and years, but mercifully, for most of us, they wane in intensity over time. When we nurture grief, as a natural part of life, it passes like winter into spring. When we fail to take care of it, not only sadness, but all our emotions can become numbed. Repressed grief dampens our joy, withers trust, and feeds guilt, as if survival itself is shameful. Unless we express it and treat it tenderly, grief can create chronic pain.

The Balm of Acceptance

Mercifully, most grieving people do eventually arrive at a shore of acceptance. Sometimes this virtue appears surprisingly early in those who are dying.

People die the way they lived. They respond to the prospect of their own death the way they have always responded to life and its challenges. If they have been repeatedly hurt, this is yet another blow. Others experience a sense of despairing finality, as if the sudden confrontation with their own mortality confirms an old belief that life cannot be trusted. Some individuals, who are typically argumentative or demanding in the midst of their control issues, become even more controlling as they face the end of life.

In John's case, because of his lifelong virtue of optimism, death became yet another novel experience to be fully explored. I had never seen him cry since his diagnosis, until one day when I found him in tears. Fortunately, I remembered to use the Virtues Project strategy of Companioning, a practice of compassionate presence allowing others to fully express their feelings. I refrained from sympathizing with what I assumed was his recognition of how terribly tragic this whole thing was – which can often seem like an imposition to the person who is crying. Instead, I asked an open-ended "cup emptying" question, "What are those tears?" as I reached out and held him. "It's so beautiful," he said, having read spiritual texts about life after death throughout the morning. "The next world is so beautiful." He gently let go of me, and dried his eyes, saying. "I've decided. This is an adventure." John's strong faith was a portal to grace, giving him a lens to view dying as a trip to "Adventure Land" rather than just mourning what was being lost. What fitting creativity for a Disney imagineer. It was all I could do to meet him in that place of ready openness – that "vibrant relationship with the unknown".

Years before, he had said something that I liked so much I quoted it in my daily meditation book, Sacred Moments, under the virtue of Grace:

When one is going through major change, a new job, a new life, there is a lot of fear of the unknowns. It's like kayaking on white water. You're paddling. You're upright. There's speed, beauty, and a sense of grace. And at any moment, you could turn a corner, lose your balance, and turn over. Meanwhile, all you do is keep paddling and remain upright.

As he faced his own death, John faithfully embodied the spirit of these words. He chose conscious dying: seeing it as an opportunity to slow down into awareness, to meet the turns and surprises of his illness with curiosity, with gratitude for the gifts of his life. He lived fully until the very end.

"To spare oneself from grief at all costs can be achieved only at the price of total detachment, which excludes the ability to experience happiness."
Erich Fromm, psychologist and author

SUSTAINING VIRTUES:

Acceptance – Embracing life on its own terms. Acceptance allows us to bend without breaking in the face of tests.

Flexibility – The ability to adapt and change amidst the fluctuating circumstances of life. Everything changes in the dying process. We need to go with the flow.

HEALING STEPS:

1. Expect change as the only constant in your journey of grief. It will help you to develop the resilience you need.

2. Give your grief a voice. Naming the phases and faces of grief, and sharing it with others who know its contours, can help to alleviate the pain or at least not leave you speechless, alone and isolated.

3 LOSSES AND LITTLE DEATHS

"I bend but do not break."

Jean de la Fontaine, 17th century French poet

The day one receives a terminal diagnosis, "life as we know it" is over, never, ever to return. The disappearance of normalcy is only the first of many losses and little deaths that the dying and their intimates have to face.

Until it is lost to us, the sense of "life as usual", awakening to a casual curiosity about what a new day will bring, is a gift we tend to take for granted. Impending death overshadows everything, and we are catapulted into the realm of the unknown. What's going to happen? Will there be pain? When will death occur? How can we possibly prepare for it? The only thing we can count on is change.

A Change of Roles

From the slam of anticipatory grief to a sense of abandonment before and after our loved one dies, the little deaths continue for those of us being left behind. Often, for those closest to the dying person, particularly a life partner, the relationship instantly changes from someone we have leaned on to someone who now needs our care. This is a huge adjustment for everyone. If the one who is dying has done all the cooking, the finances, the holiday planning, the gradual loss of these life skills severely threatens their sense of purpose.

When we take on the role of caregiver, we need to be aware of how painful it can be for the individual whose dependence is increasing. They have in essence lost their life's work. No matter how tasty your scrambled eggs may be, don't be surprised if they try to tell you how to do it better, or grumble under their breath about how they always did them differently. Irritability over little things is one expression of their grief and needs to be taken compassionately. Please do your best not to take it personally. Just acknowledge it without necessarily trying to fix anything.

Who Am I Now?

As a dying person's powers and capacities fade and ebb, and increasing physical changes occur, a spiritual crisis often arises – loss of the sense of self as one has been known in the world. From the death of one's dreams for the future to decreasing mobility, it is common to experience the diminishment of one's personhood. An increasing loss of independence may be the most grievous loss, as it threatens a huge part of one's persona, one's very identity.

I remember visiting a woman in hospice dying of cancer, who was grieving deeply. When I companioned her about her tears, she said, "It's just so hard." "What's hard?" I asked. "Everyone taking care of me. I just can't stand it." As she shared her story, it was clear that she was the one who had looked after everyone else in the family. In losing this role, she lost herself – her sense of her own value. Thankfully, I knew not to say something inane like, "Now it's your turn, honey. It's about time someone took care of you." What I did acknowledge was her lifelong generosity to her family. "It's really hard when you are the one who has always taken care of everyone else."

Driving Dependency

It is a huge blow when someone cannot drive any longer. For many men, their car is an extension of themselves. And every time they want to go somewhere, they have to ask to be taken. John at times felt guilty because he loved to be out and about, and that meant our driving him around, sometimes every day. Dan continually assured him, "This is what we're here for, John." John's ability to walk unaided would come and go. Several times he had to give in and start using a walker. One time when he had temporarily regained sufficient stability to walk unaided, he asked us to return the wheel chair and walker we had gotten from the Red Cross. Perhaps this was a way to sustain the illusion that he was "better now" and wouldn't need those blasted contraptions again. We removed them from his sight, but kept them in a corner of the garage until they were needed once again a few weeks later.

Body Image

The loss of hair, a breast, changes in weight loss or gain, are profound blows to one's body image. All his life, John had been fit and slim, having walked miles every day through the theme parks where he worked for Disney. John always walked so fast that I could never keep up with him. Now I was holding him up to cross the street.

Because he was on increasing steroid doses, he had gained sixty pounds and looked like a sweet-faced Santa with a beach ball belly. One time, when I was driving him to meet some friends for lunch, he sighed and said, "I wish I weren't so vain. This is really hard." "Do you miss your slim self?", I asked. Then, I said something that seemed to comfort him greatly. "John, this isn't about vanity. It's about identity." "Oh, that's true," he said. "Thank you." The validation of this loss seemed to give him some relief. We need to be careful not to rationalize away these small losses, although I confess, I then added. "You're still gorgeous."

The Dignity Factor

As the need to be cared for increases, the dying person may develop a sense of humiliation. When they must depend on family members or professional caregivers for personal care – washing, toileting, or dressing, a matter of fact attitude is essential. A "no big deal" joking attitude is sometimes the most helpful. John got to the point where he had to wear adult diapers at night. "Why should you complain?" I'd say, "I had to wear them every month most of my life." Often, the individual's need for dignity is best served by a professional caregiver coming in to take care of these intimate needs rather than a family member.

Financial Loss

For many individuals, the loss of income is devastating. I have actually never encountered an individual who was afraid of death itself but many were very troubled about how their loved ones would survive without them. For this reason, it is important for everyone, as we get older, to do end of life planning, including survivor benefits.

Touch Me
At some point during a terminal illness, there is also the loss of sex. There must not be loss of touch. Many dying individuals become skin hungry. They need to be held, touched, or massaged. They will show you if they do not want to be touched. Reach out, and be prepared to pull back as well.

I found that patients in hospice loved to have their hands massaged with lotion. One man seemed comatose, but when I stopped, he came drifting up to consciousness, and said, "Don't stop," then shut his eyes and started breathing deeply and steadily again. One of my spiritual care volunteers at hospice, a tiny elderly woman, would climb onto the bed and rock the person. She also offered what she called, "Sacred Massage." She prayed silently for the person as she touched them. She brought amazing peace to people. She taught the rest of our spiritual care volunteers that if you massage the feet, you are asking the person to stay, and if you stroke their head, you are giving them permission to go.

Abandonment Revisited
The losses of the ones being left behind continue to expand and deepen as well. Not only did I lose my confidant, the one with whom I would normally share my every thought and feeling; in John's case, he was also my social companion with our friends, and my treasured co-worker as designer of what we called "our legacy line" for The Virtues Project. The first time he tried, and failed, to correct a simple design on a new poster, he turned pale. He said, "I just can't." When I was alone, I wept for this loss of competence John was experiencing, and for my own loss of this cherished partnership in working for the Project Dan, John and I had birthed together.

For John, of course, the loss of his capacities as a productive doer was profound. Yet, somehow he found the strength to surrender to each loss. For him, it wasn't about giving up. He had a sense of awe at the new crop of gentler virtues enriching his inner life – acceptance, prayerfulness, openness, and gratitude, among them.

To survive the journey of grief, we must open to it. We need to prepare ourselves for multiple losses and accept change as the new normal.

"When you are sorrowful look again in your heart, and you shall see that in truth you are weeping for that which has been your delight."
Khalil Gibran, Lebanese-American poet, artist & author

SUSTAINING VIRTUES:

Endurance – our ability to withstand adversity and hardship. We practice perseverance and patience when obstacles arise, open to the lessons they bring. Endurance gives us the strength to stay the course.

Forbearance – Tolerating hardship with good grace. Not allowing the trials of life to steal our joy.

HEALING STEPS:

1. Call on the strength of endurance to face every change. It will help you to avoid being blind-sided by the shifting realities of symptoms as they come and go, then come again – a typical pattern in brain cancer and other terminal illnesses.

2. Be a safe place for your loved one to lean. Be open to whatever they are feeling, and when listening to them, put on a shield over your heart of Compassion and Detachment, so you can walk intimately with them without being devastated by their feelings. Let them tell you their true story as it unfolds.

4 GONE TOO SOON

"A sudden tragic event shatters our sense of order and thrusts us into a world forever changed."
www.journeyofhearts.org

The experience of a sudden death through an accident, a heart attack, or a suicide can be devastating. There are no words to describe the swirling, complex layers of shock, numbness, sadness, despair, guilt and anger that such an event brings in its wake. There is no time to say goodbye, to resolve anything, to prepare for this devastating loss. Trust is wrenched out from under us, leaving us utterly traumatized. Grief is even more traumatic when the death is a result of suicide.

In the Wake of Suicide

It is almost inevitable after a cherished person dies to have regrets, and wonder if one could have done more for the person. After a suicide, there is a deadly combination of anger at the person who chose to die, and at oneself for not being able to save them. Grief is compounded by regret, guilt, and helplessness. I strongly recommend that anyone who has suffered this kind of loss get professional help.

Truthfully, we are never responsible for another's life or death, even that of our child. As a therapist, I specialized in suicide prevention and intervention. In working with people who had failed in their suicide attempts, I found that often, a suicide was an ultimate act of revenge for a hurt, a gesture of rage, meant to have a huge impact on someone in their lives. One woman said of a lover who had rejected her, "I wanted to leave my corpse on his doorstep." We played out the scene in fantasy until she laughed with glee. We then traced the origins of her violent reaction to rejection back to her childhood. She said it was like uncoiling the tangled film of her life, and rewinding it on its spool until it made sense. She was then free to live for herself.

In the aftermath of a suicide, to stop living is a meaningless sacrifice. We need to somehow carry on, although it is essential to invest the time to empty one's cup of remorse and grief first. Otherwise one is only half alive. Death has conquered both the departed and those left behind. Others in our lives need to understand and be patient as we undertake the long journey of grieving.

Losing a Child

Perhaps the most tragic loss of all is the death of a child. It is like a promise betrayed, an inexplicable disappearance. The vacancy left in the heart and arms of a parent is profound. It affects the lives of surviving siblings deeply as well. The death of a child leaves in its wake multiple losses of "what could have been." One will never get to watch them grow, applaud at their graduation, see them marry. The future is utterly bereft.

There is great danger of harboring a needless loss as well. The memory of the lost child is often enshrined and idealized by parents, leaving the living child feeling forever diminished. How can they ever measure up? This is a challenge for any family, one that is worthy of great effort, both to navigate the journey of grief, and to focus lovingly on the living at the same time.

Multiple Losses

I met a woman who could write the book on multiple, sudden losses. When she was fifteen, she had been asked to look after her grandmother while her parents were in town shopping. She recalls bringing her a cup of tea, then settling in to watch Lassie on television. She suddenly jumped up, with a strange awareness, went to see how her grandmother was, and found her constant companion, a large Rottweiler, in her room alone. She ran down to the nearby dam, and found her grandmother floating in the deep water, obviously dead. She sank to her knees and screamed, bringing siblings running. She yelled to them to stay away but could not bring herself to retrieve the body. The aftermath of guilt was terrible, and the sadness at realizing her grandmother had committed suicide after a stroke has lasted decades. "You never get over it," she said. Her younger brother, was killed at age 11 by a car, and her older brother, a biker gang member, was shot to death.

I asked her how she had lived through it all. She said she became a critical care nurse. Then, she said, "Hmm, I wonder if these losses had anything to do with it." Finding a way to be of service to others who are suffering is a redemptive and healing choice. At the time I met her, she was a happy, fulfilled woman, an artist and a massage therapist with a deeply compassionate presence. There are many wounded healers who have taken a path in life to support the wellbeing of others.

What We Need
What we most need at a time of abrupt or tragic loss is an enveloping blanket of love and support, including people who have the fortitude to listen to whatever we are feeling and the patience to care for a very, very long time. We need someone to serve as a compassionate witness to our harsh grief, to literally offer a crying towel for our tears, and deliver food, so we will eat. Grief of this nature really takes its time.

"Help us to be always the hopeful gardeners of the spirit
who know that without darkness
nothing comes to birth
as without light
nothing flowers."
May Sarton, American poet & novelist

SUSTAINING VIRTUES:

Patience is quiet hope and faith that things will turn out right. We trust the process of life. We do not rush or allow ourselves to be overcome by pressure. Patience helps us to endure things we cannot control. It soothes our souls, and helps us to get through the emotional floodtide as it moves and changes.

I believe that men need a unique approach to healing grief. They too, need to learn to befriend their pain, to open themselves to it, to soften their hearts in compassion for themselves. Yet, because they have different coping mechanisms from women, they need their own tools for the journey.

Managing Grief

There are several successful strategies to help men live through the experience of grief:

1. Realize it IS a journey, not a vortex of whirling chaotic emotion from which you will never emerge. You need to make your own map, like John's emergence from his first foray into grief, deciding to view terminal illness as a new adventure.

2. Take whatever space necessary to go inside and feel the grief, to chip away at it in contained, manageable bits. You may need to listen to music – whatever helps you get to your feelings. Golden calls this "sampling" the grief. Many older men find themselves weeping easily and seem mystified by it. I believe this phenomenon results from decades of unshed tears. Best to let them out gently in the face of grief.

3. Create a ritual to make grief manageable. For example, at a certain time of day in a private place to take out the photo of your loved one, and allow the grief to surface as it will, releasing your tears, or yelling out your rage. I was once asked by a New Zealand Maori man in his thirties to companion him. He had had three heart attacks. "What's breaking your heart?" I asked him, and he said that his older brother had committed suicide that year. "I just can't let him go." Together we designed a release ritual of a homemade raft carrying one of his brother's belongings. At the next full moon, he brought it to the ocean and let it go.

4. Men need the companionship of other grieving men, ideally with a male counselor to guide the process. I have had the privilege of working with grieving men in groups and find that

they are an amazing support to one another, even holding one another tenderly when one gets to his tears.

5. Gotta Move. I have also learned from the men in my life, including those I saw as a psychotherapist, that to access their feelings, they need to be moving. When my sons were young, and I sensed something was troubling them, I couldn't get them to talk to me about it until I took them for a drive. As the wheels were turning, they would start talking. A high school teacher who is also a Virtues Project facilitator said that he never sits across from a male student to talk about a problem or aggressive behavior. He takes a walk with him. "It has to be shoulder to shoulder, not eye to eye," he said. I have always followed this rule with my husband Dan when I felt we needed to talk. To him, this was a "meta-conversation" – a talk about talking, relating about relationship – which he would have much preferred to skip altogether. Yet, as we walk, he does talk.

6. Men often need physical ways to express grief – carving, painting, building something in the loved one's name. In one First Nation group of severely abused men, Kevin spoke of a dark hole inside that started when he was a battered, sexually abused child. I gave him a large piece of paper and asked him to draw the hole. He sat on the floor and put stroke after violent stroke of black marker on that entire paper. He and all of us wept with him as he drew. We then went outside, wadded the paper up in a can and burned it. Kevin and I walked across a field to put the ashes at the root of a rose bush, but when we got there, the can was mysteriously empty. He ran back to the circle of men whooping with joy.

"Joy and grief are brothers in a way, and if you experience one fully
you will probably experience the other in its fullness."
Tom Golden, grief counselor

SUSTAINING VIRTUES:

Courage allows us to face adversity with confidence. Courage gives me the strength to make this journey with all my heart.

Tolerance helps us be open to differences and frees us from being judgmental. It is an appreciation for diversity, whether of culture or temperament. It leads to unity. Tolerance is accepting things that we wish were different with humor and grace. It allows us to embrace the pain as well as the joys of life.

HEALING STEPS:

1. Men need great courage to find their way through unaccustomed assaults of emotion. They need to avoid self-destructive actions and instead reach out for help, particularly from other men.

2. For women, it takes great tolerance and empathy to accept a man's way of grieving. Giving genuine support means respecting his space, avoiding advice, and just listening silently when he does speak of his grief. Then acknowledge his courage or endurance. Men need tolerance as well, to allow a woman her own way of swimming through the currents of grief.

II VIRTUES FOR THE JOURNEY

"Virtue is the muscle tone in the daily and hourly training of a spiritual warrior."
Tolbert McCarroll, Prior, Starcross monastic community

When facing our own death or that of someone we love, it is not uncommon for a swirling, overwhelming chaos to envelop us. What if we had a rope to grab, a trail guide, a way to help each other create a path through grief?

The Five Strategies of The Virtues Project offer a template for transformational living. They are spiritual life skills, to use throughout life. Our family found them deeply helpful tools in facing the ordeal of dying and loss. They not only helped us as survival strategies but gifted us with a rich and vital experience.

As John's chosen caregivers, Dan and I provided a safe environment within which he lived as full a life as possible. We fed him, advocated for his medical needs, administered his finances under his guidance, did his laundry, and took on all his responsibilities when he was ready or forced by his illness to release them. We were his willing chauffeurs. We granted his last wishes as best we could. Above all what was most meaningful to him was that we companioned him on his spiritual journey.

We stepped away from our own lives for this time of caring, which blessed us as much as it did John. He often thanked us tearfully for making his last days so special.

Looking back on the last fifteen months of John's life, I know that the Virtues Strategies we had been teaching and living for years as the three founders, became a sacred structure within which John found a depth of freedom to experience his feelings, speak his truth, reflect on his life, and to move, as he put it, "from doing to being", with a surprising and profound sense of joy.

My hope in sharing these strategies with those of you who are facing the end of life, as persons living with death, or the ones caring for them, is that they will bring you a measure of grace, as they did for us.

VIRTUES: THE GIFTS OF CHARACTER

Acceptance	Faithfulness	Patience
Accountability	Fidelity	Peacefulness
Appreciation	Flexibility	Perceptiveness
Assertiveness	Forbearance	Perseverance
Awe	Forgiveness	Prayerfulness
Beauty	Fortitude	Purity
Caring	Friendliness	Purposefulness
Certitude	Generosity	Reliability
Charity	Gentleness	Resilience
Cheerfulness	Grace	Respect
Cleanliness	Gratitude	Responsibility
Commitment	Helpfulness	Reverence
Compassion	Honesty	Righteousness
Confidence	Honor	Sacrifice
Consideration	Hope	Self-discipline
Contentment	Humanity	Serenity
Cooperation	Humility	Service
Courage	Idealism	Simplicity
Courtesy	Independence	Sincerity
Creativity	Initiative	Steadfastness
Decisiveness	Integrity	Strength
Detachment	Joyfulness	Tact
Determination	Justice	Thankfulness
Devotion	Kindness	Thoughtfulness
Dignity	Love	Tolerance
Diligence	Loyalty	Trust
Discernment	Mercy	Trustworthiness
Empathy	Mindfulness	Truthfulness
Endurance	Moderation	Understanding
Enthusiasm	Modesty	Unity
Excellence	Nobility	Wisdom
Fairness	Openness	Wonder
Faith	Optimism	Zeal
	Orderliness	

FIVE VIRTUES STRATEGIES
FOR END OF LIFE

The Five Strategies of The Virtues Project are practices that bring virtues to life. They help us to live authentic, purposeful lives, to raise children of compassion and idealism, and to create a culture of character in our schools and communities. In the journey of grief and death, they are tools for navigating with grace. Here is an overview, followed by a chapter on each strategy.

Strategy 1 – Speaking the Language of Virtues

Language has the power to discourage or to inspire. The Language of Virtues is a vocabulary of love and meaning that affirms others. It is a way to acknowledge, correct, and thank. At the end of life, it gives us specific terms for thanking others and saying goodbye. It is also a tactful but powerful way to avoid criticizing while requesting correction or changes in behavior.

Virtues are a frame of reference – or more accurately, a frame of reverence for life – a way of thinking, being, acting and speaking that brings strength and hope as we grieve. It is a way to make our choices in the most meaningful way. It is the oldest language of the world, found in all the world's sacred texts. It contains the words that describe our spiritual essence.

"Your patience is amazing." "What gives you this serenity?" "Speaking to your aunt on the phone would be a kind thing to do." "Please use your tact when you aren't happy with something I'm doing." "Thank you for your faithful friendship."

Strategy 2 – Recognizing Teachable Moments

Life is school, and everything that happens is for our learning. At any point in time, we have both strength virtues that are well developed and growth virtues that we need to develop. Recognizing the virtues in which we need to grow, especially in painful or challenging situations, helps us to live mindfully, to be lifelong learners, open to our soul work – that which gives us meaning and purpose. It is an attitude that keeps us from shaming ourselves or dwelling on guilt. We use guilt only as a signal for change. We call on the virtues that can heal our wounds, enrich our relationships, and help us to make amends after a mistake. Being open to teachable moments prepares us to face whatever happens with receptivity to grace.

"What virtue do I need now?" "What would give me the endurance to live through this?" "What do I need in order to find forgiveness for my father?" "What is the gift in this illness?" "How do I prepare for death?" "How do I lovingly care for my grief?"

Strategy 3 – Setting Clear Boundaries

Setting boundaries based on respect and restorative justice creates a climate of peace, unity, and safety. We are clear about what we are willing or not willing to do in a situation, and what we will or will not tolerate from others. Boundaries guard our time and our energy. When facing loss and death, we need boundaries that protect the needs and rights of the dying person and everyone involved. We need a just approach to resolving inevitable family conflicts. Virtues-based boundaries guide us through the difficult end of life decisions. They help caregivers to remember self-care. They nurture family unity at a critical and sensitive time by focusing on what is right and needful under the circumstances.

"I need to decide who I feel comfortable seeing." "How do I schedule my day of caregiving to get enough rest?" "When is enough chemo enough?" "As I write my will, how can I be considerate and fair to those left behind?" "What will free me as a caregiver to obtain respite care for my loved one, so that I can take a break?"

Strategy 4 – Honoring the Spirit

Honoring the spirit means first of all preserving the dignity of each person, with courtesy, kindness and respect. It also involves daily spiritual practices, such as a routine of reverence, which can be the heart of the dying and grieving process. It is planning personalized ceremonies, integrating virtues into our daily activities. After death occurs, it is creating a meaningful celebration of life. Paying tribute to the virtues of a loved one is the primary way people of all cultures honor their dead.

"Who needs to hear from me and how can I acknowledge them before I die?" "What would I find inspiring to read or listen to in my daily sacred time?" "How can we design a personal celebration of life that really honors our loved one?" "Shall we celebrate while they are still alive and able to witness it?"

Strategy 5 – Offering Spiritual Companioning

Being deeply present and listening with compassionate curiosity supports individuals to heal during the journey of grief. Cup-emptying "What" and "How" questions allow the dying and the grieving a safe outlet for their tears and whatever they are feeling. Companioning provides an opening for the dying to do their life review and to make end of life decisions. It is a gift we can give one another that helps us to accept our feelings, our losses and our victories as well. It is the single most important tool caregivers have to offer the dying and the bereaved.

"What's on your mind today?" "What's the hardest thing about this?" "What is your deepest feeling today?" "What gives you comfort?" "What are you proudest of in your life?" "What are you grateful for?"

6 THE LANGUAGE OF LOVE

"How can you tell someone loves you?" "By the way they say your name. You know your name is safe in their mouth."
A 4 year old interviewed by author, Leo Bascaglia

It's important to tell the people we love that we love them. It is even more important to tell them what we love about them, by speaking the Language of Virtues. When my father was dying, he gave me and my brothers, John and Tommy, a great gift. He gathered us around him, and told us, for the first time in our lives, what he admired about each of us. He started with me, and said, "Linda, you are my strongest child." My father's words were a source of deep encouragement in the following years, when The Virtues Project took me and Dan into cities, jungles, and remote villages throughout the world.

That day, as he sat spent and exhausted after speaking to us, he beckoned me over for a brief, urgent epilogue. "Lin, be yourself. Be yourself. Be yourself." "What do you mean, Dad? Do you think I'm not myself?" "No, but sometimes you're more than yourself." That lesson came back to me years later when, in meditation, I heard, "Linda, you are either a Mack truck or as gentle as a deer. Your power is in your gentleness." As I continued my walking meditation on the gravel road through the pine forest near our home that day, I suddenly heard a roaring noise, and a Mack truck sped by me. A few minutes later, a deer stepped out of the woods and just stared at me with its limpid brown eyes. God always does the timing.
My father's reference to the balancing virtues of Strength and Gentleness was a life-changing moment – one that has guided me over the years, when I remember it.

Mirror the Virtues You See
When I served as Spiritual Care Director for Hospice in the 1980's, I found that when I acknowledged dying persons for virtues at the end of our visits, their faces would softly illuminate with joy. One time, I companioned a frail man in his last hours and he poured out to me the horrors of his day and made it clear he just wanted to

death, we open to the wonder in this exquisite and fragile existence.

HEALING STEPS:

1. When you are with someone who is dying, don't be a jewel thief, stealing away their teachable moments out of misguided compassion. Don't try to supply answers to their questions, or God forbid, instant "wisdom sayings", which are about as palatable as instant coffee. Don't rationalize away their imminent demise. Instead, give them questions that help them to discover the heart of the matter in their teachable moments. Sit with them in their puzzlement, their holy confusion.

2. Have the curiosity to be open to the many new learnings that only grief and loss can bring. These gifts may, one day, seem worth everything you have gone through.

8 NEEDFUL BOUNDARIES

"You are your only master, who else?"
The Dhammapada of Buddhism

People who live without setting clear personal boundaries can easily lose themselves to the people and the work they love. One can easily drift from being helpful to being codependent, which is an addictive need to be needed. It is all too easy for the caregiver of a dying person to relinquish all limits and sacrifice too much for too long.

Boundaries are essential for intimacy without enmeshment, to avoid sliding into co-dependence, which has a huge ingredient of control. Of course I know nothing about that!

Decide What You Can Give
Our situation was a rare one. Dan and I could afford to give up a few months of our lives to care for John directly. Our children were grown. Our work was flexible. And we knew John's brain cancer was an aggressive one, and that he did not have that long to live. Everyone faced with the terminal illness of a loved one needs to discern the boundaries of their care-giving. What can they give to their loved one without becoming utterly overwhelmed or jeopardizing their own health, their work or family life? When does the dying person need professional care and what part can a family member realistically play?

When is Caring Co-dependence?
A caregiver needs to be open to learning the difference between control, catering and caring. Dan and I did lots of catering, and were happy to do it. We were our own "Make a wish" foundation for John. But the difference between control and caring only became clear as John's boundaries developed.

Truthfully, I felt at times as if John and I had merged. He would often say, "Lin, you seem to read my mind about what I need. How do you do that?" My first priority was to do everything, and be everything he needed. Yet, when one is this close to another, it is easy to transgress an unseen boundary, from which we must step back, to protect their fragile sense of independence and dignity, so essential until the very end.

The tricky thing about boundaries is that often we don't know what they are until we trip over them, or step over the line. A sudden burst of anger is often the signal that a boundary has been violated. Sometimes a dying person can become explosively angry, seemingly out of the blue. I was told by a counsellor at the Cancer Centre that this is particularly true of individuals with brain cancer, who apparently develop rigidity, because it is so hard to feel helplessly out of control when something is destroying their very brain.

This happened only twice with John. The first time, he was in the hospital following his second surgery and he wanted to shave using his electric razor. He was having trouble getting it to work, and as the one who helped him with everything, I took the shaver and fiddled with it, trying to get it working – even though I am utterly non-mechanical. John used to say I was "physics-ly challenged". He grabbed it back and just kept turning it over and over. I ached to see him so frustrated. Later, the same day, at John's request, Dan and I drove several miles away to find a Dairy Queen. We brought John out to a visiting area in a wheelchair to enjoy his ice cream. When he finished, he began to lecture me soundly, in front of Dan, about what an interfering person I was, that I always thought I knew better than anyone else. It was like being punched in the solar plexus. I could hardly breathe. This from the person who thanked me over and over for tending to his needs. Others, whose intimates died of cancer, have shared with me their deep hurt by outbursts like this.

The way I got through it was to reflect on what had happened as a teachable moment, seeking to discern the message John was sending. This competent man who had designed, constructed and managed countless projects was now baffled by everyday mechanics. Even though he could not articulate it, his boundary was clear. "Do not help me with mechanical things." He preferred to puzzle and struggle. I had to step back whenever this happened with the television remote, or his I-Pod, or the coffee pot. Thankfully, once I got the message, harmony was restored.

A few months later, when his alarm clock "broke" from his random button pushing, I breezily said, "Let's go shopping for a new one today, John. Would you like that?" He flared up once again. "Linda, let me decide what I'm going to buy and when!" I thought, "No, I won't accept this." John had violated a boundary of mine, by misinterpreting my motives as control rather than care. I felt it was simply unjust and I needed to clear it up. I said, "John, I hear you about needing to make these decisions yourself, and I will respect that. And when you talk to me, you have to be kind. You have to be kind." His eyes widened, as if realizing this small injustice. "I'm sorry, Lin," he said. That was the last time he spoke to me without tact, and the last time I presumed to make any decisions at all that he could make for himself, even if a bright idea presented itself. His dignity was more important.

Excess or Success in Caregiving
Generosity often trumps wisdom when we offer our hearts, our service, our time and our energy. Natural caregivers are particularly prone to sacrifice self for the other. So, unless we consciously consider and set boundaries, we will exceed our own limits, and suffer the inevitable exhaustion of attempting to do too much by ourselves.

I learned the hard way that I had waited too long to get help. A few weeks before John died, we hired a marvellous woman who was very experienced in home care for the dying, but she was only available one day a week. At least I could take real breathers during the few hours she came. However, it took a visit to the emergency room with a pseudo heart attack for me to realize I had to bring in help in John's last restless nights. I waited so long, however, that on the very day a home care worker was to begin the night shift, John died.

Guarding Privacy
In facing the end of life, the dying person has a whole new lifestyle
to get used to. A continually shifting new normal calls for careful
discernment of boundaries to protect vanishing energy. There is
often a deeper need for privacy, as bodily challenges increase. How
can their dignity be protected when they need someone to wipe
their bottom, to change their sheets daily, to get them in and out of
the tub? For some, a family member is the best person to do this.
For others, their dignity demands that a professional be brought in
to do these things. Alternatively, if much physical care is needed,
that often requires a move to a nursing facility, hospital or hospice.

Boundaries need to be continually considered as the individual
weakens and needs more sleep and less stimulation. Many well-
meaning people actually offered to come and live in John's house,
people who were mere acquaintances! One woman insisted on
flying to our island to bring John bottles and jars of her homemade
concoctions. She had never met us but had taken a course in The
Virtues Project. She said God told her to come and hold John and
he would be healed. She went to the doors of our neighbours, to
ask their advice about getting in to see him, despite my telling her
on one of her many phone calls that our family needed privacy
now. Finally the police became involved when a neighbor reported
her. John called her "the virtues stalker" and was very upset by this
intrusion. I later surmised that she was a woman in a manic state
of manic depressive illness. She meant well but she caused great
dismay. I had to set very strong boundaries that she could not come
to the house or contact us again.

As his energy waned, I would ask John if there was anyone he
wanted to see. He would get very quiet, think about it, and then
I would write down the short list of names, some of whom were
quite surprising. People who visit need to be very respectful of the
boundaries around visiting, around touch, around how long to stay.
If someone was not a hugger or hand holder before they became
ill, they may not want to be now. Or maybe they do. The key is to
follow their cues, to sense their need for physical space or closeness.

The purpose of boundaries is not to limit us but to guard our freedom, to allow us to stand on our own holy ground. It also gives others clarity about what we need, what we stand for, and what we won't stand for. Boundaries give us a sense of safety and trust in our relationships, helping us to understand each other's needs.

> *"Out beyond ideas of wrongdoing and right-doing, there is a field.*
> *I'll meet you there."*
> Jalal'u'din Rumi, Sufi mystic poet

SUSTAINING VIRTUES:

Assertiveness is speaking one's truth with peaceful confidence. We tell the truth about what is just. Assertiveness comes from knowing our own worth, and honoring the dignity of who we are. We set boundaries without guilt.

Respect is an attitude of honoring ourselves and others as people of value. We care for each person's dignity. Everyone has the right to expect respect. We show respect in the courtesy of our words, and in our tone of voice. We are all exquisitely sensitive to respect. It helps us to discern the boundaries that each person needs to feel loved and supported.

HEALING STEPS:

1. At each phase of illness and dying, take time to reflect on what boundaries are called for, in order to respect the individual's dignity and independence.

2. As a caregiver, notice when you are approaching compassion fatigue, and get some respite care, sooner rather than later. Recognize when it is time to bring in professional help for personal care.

a pure heart."

I actively companioned him during the meditative, reflective portion. I would ask open-ended questions such as, "What's on your mind today, John?" He would sit back, close his eyes, and say, "Hmm." Then he would speak and sometimes weep. Most of the time, for John, they were tears of gratitude for his rich life, especially his opportunities to be of service.

During these sacred mornings, he reflected deeply. He often said that our shared routine of reverence was the heart of his spiritual life now, the chalice for his conscious dying.

I found his reflections so powerful and eloquent at times that I asked if he would mind if I recorded him. Actually, I think it pleased him. One morning he began to speak about the samurai sword, and the powerful excellence of its artisan, likening that to how God molds us, puts us in the fires of tests, not to harm us but to refine and strengthen us. John went on to talk more about God's refining fire. "What's impressive is the skill of the artisan, and the heat he has to suffer as he crafts that sword. He turns it back on itself. The metal itself is reconstituted into a new form. It's incredibly strong. If we are faithful to God's teachings, we become a new being."

The final step in our routine was for each of us to do a Virtues Pick using Virtues Reflection Cards. John reached into the Japanese kimono bag (which he designed and arranged to import), randomly picked a virtue card, and read it aloud. As his vision faded, he asked me to read his card. He would then share how it spoke to him. This required silent companioning, which gave him all the space he needed for reflection without interruption. When he was finished, I gave him virtues acknowledgments, for his peacefulness, his acceptance, or his joyfulness. Then I would do my own pick. And what delightful, touching acknowledgments he would give me. One morning, he said, "I've been thinking Linda, what you are to me. You're like the blue angel spreading peace and joy." I knew he was

referring to the image of the angelic fairy in Pinocchio. A sweet gift
I will never forget.

Make Space for Life Review
Sometimes our sacred mornings took more than an hour,
particularly when we would story together about our lives. It
gave him an opening to do his life review. He would talk about his
proudest accomplishments, his wishes, his joys, and most of all his
gratitude. He was so thankful for the times when he was able to
create something new or to be of service to the Baha'i Faith or to
The Virtues Project.

John recounted moments when he took on a design challenge such
as the 1993 Baha'i World Congress at the Jacob Javitz Center in
New York. He had telephoned me one day, saying . "Lin, I'm stuck.
It's a very complex design and it just isn't coming." So, I reminded
him of the presence of his A-Team – ancestors, angels and advisors
in the spiritual realm. "Who in the next world do you admire for
design, someone you could call on?" He immediately answered,
"I've always admired Frank Lloyd Wright". Later that day, he went
into a book store and his eye went immediately to a rare book of
designs by Wright, including stained glass illustrations. Wright
said, "Form follows function - that has been misunderstood. Form
and function should be one, joined in a spiritual union." Wright
provided John's inspiration for the jewel colors and the brilliant
construction elements for the conference.

Life review is one of the primary soul tasks for all of us as we face
the end of life, and most dying people I have known do a life review
in one way or another. This is a time to listen deeply, without fixing,
advising, or over-sympathizing. Bring only your compassionate
curiosity to hear their stories and listen for the meaning in them.
This is not only an approach that helps to honor the spirit: it is as
well the essence of the fifth strategy, Offer Spiritual Companioning.
It gives meaning and illumination to the dying and detaching
process.

"Life is not measured by the number of breaths we take
but by the moments that take our breath away."
Author unknown

SUSTAINING VIRTUES:

Reverence is nurturing our inner life. It is living with an awareness that we are always in the presence of the Creator and that all life is precious. We open ourselves to experience faith, love and deep respect for the mysteries and wonders of life. We take time in solitude and silence each day to contemplate, to pray and reflect. We seek to discern the deeper meaning of our lives. When we are facing the end of life, taking sacred time each day is a way to explore the meaning and gifts of our life. Reverence consecrates our lives.

Grace is our connection to the Divine, a sense that we are loved and provided for in all circumstances. We cultivate grace by opening ourselves to bounty. Grace inspires us to give unconditional love to others. It is the willingness to forgive. With grace, we can turn every communication and relationship into a thing of beauty. As we connect deeply with grace, we become the presence of grace to others.

HEALING STEPS:

1. As a caregiver, give time and deep attention to the spiritual needs of the dying person. This opens a space for them to do their soul work of preparing for the end of life.

2. To the extent that you both are comfortable, set up a regular routine giving space to the individual to talk or reflect, even if just "time to chat". If the notion of RPMS fits for you, take the time to do a full routine of reverence together. It is far more important than the myriad physical tasks involved in caring for the dying.

3. Be sure not to interrupt with well-meaning advice, reassurances, or cheery sayings when someone is opening to the deep questions that arise at the end of life. Appreciate the privilege of being there to witness them entering sacred territory.

4. After listening, remember to give virtues acknowledgments.

10 COMPASSIONATE PRESENCE

"Listening is a magnetic and strange thing, a creative force. The friends who listen to us are the ones we move toward. When we are listened to, it creates us, makes us unfold and expand."
Karl Menninger, American psychiatrist

When someone is in pain, our compassion calls us to respond, to do something, to bring solace. As a psychotherapist and a companion to many dying people and their families, I have learned that doing isn't the panacea it's supposed to be. The willingness to be deeply quiet, the patience to listen with our full, accepting presence, is actually the greatest gift we have to offer.

In my own grief, both before John died and for a long time thereafter, I needed space for a cavernous sense of loss. I needed people with whom I felt safe to say what I needed to say, and cry when I needed to cry. I was shocked by how unusual it was to encounter people with the courage (or was it the skill?) to just be with me in my grief without advising, judging, or trying to jolly or rationalize me out of it.

My best friend from high school, Evelyn, knew how to be. She wept with me. She listened. What a relief to be safely vulnerable. I also spent time with a hospice volunteer who was comfortable with my tears. Dan was always there to listen, and when I felt too overwhelmed by grief, I sought the help of a psychologist who specialized in death and grief.

Practice Sacred Curiosity
I learned in my years working at Hospice that one of the greatest needs of dying people is for someone to sit beside them and be open to the reality of their experience. For many, that deep self-awareness comes only when they are free to talk with a curious, detached, compassionate person who does not shut them up with little sayings or deny the reality of their pain, their anger, or their acceptance. It is an a precious gift to anyone, at any time, to be

with them right where they are at this moment, not turning the volume up or down, but willing to ask "How are you, really?" truly interested in what is on their minds. And it is all too rare.

Never Assume

Companioning is a skill and a discipline that protects others from our assumptions about what they are feeling. This came home to me when I accompanied John to his first radiation treatment. When I asked him a companioning question as we waited – "How is this for you, John?", he admitted he had a fear of claustrophobia, knowing he would have to lie still with a mask covering his face for the radiation. "So, what would be helpful?" I asked. "Well, you're with me, and I just took an Ativan." He seemed to calm down as the moment approached, but I had a full case of the jitters, which I valiantly tried to suppress. The nurses opened a huge three foot thick steel door, and took me and John into the radiation room, with its enormous radiation machine. They laid him on a stainless steel table, and then, to my shock, bolted him down to the table with screws through the edges of his mask.

The nurses and I left, and the door clanged shut. They casually invited me to watch the procedure through their computer monitor. By this time, my heart was hammering so loud I wondered if they could hear it. Then, something went wrong. Their machine wasn't working right. They left John on the table much longer than normal as they fiddled with computer keys. I said, "Please don't leave him there. He's very claustrophobic." They said, "We have to get it right. He will just have to wait."

I had to get out of there. I couldn't bear watching him, trapped, imagining his panic, so I went back to the waiting room, praying silently. Another cancer patient said, "Who's more nervous – you or your brother?" I laughed weakly. When John came out, holding his mask, he said, "These fencing lessons aren't what they're cracked up to be!" Everyone in the waiting room laughed. He sat beside me, and said, "It didn't work. They have to do it again." I said, "How was it, John?", steeling myself for an expression of terror. "Oh, it was

them how their day was, and shared something about her own. The children hugged her and then went and played quietly, having had the affection and attention they craved. She said, "It was amazing. Usually they bug me the whole time I'm trying to cook and I end up getting mad." She had been mandated to attend the workshop after locking them in the closet, so this simple tool created a huge change for this family. Her term, "walk along" has become part of the understanding of companioning, encouraging us not to pull or push, advise or tell, but rather to walk beside others and keep them company.

"Being heard is so close to being loved that for the average person they are almost indistinguishable."
David Augsburger, author

SUSTAINING VIRTUES:

Trust: Being a helpful companion requires that we trust the process of life and death, that we hold the individual who is dying as able, knowing that this is a fragile yet powerful, potentially illuminating time for them as they face the end of this life.

Compassion and Detachment together form the shield we must put over our hearts, to avoid enmeshing with the pain of the one we are companioning. It allows us to walk intimately with another without taking on their feelings. Dying people are exquisitely sensitive, and by not being intrusive, we provide a sense of safety. This distance or space gives them the freedom to feel, to speak, to fully experience their own truth.

HEALING STEPS:

There is a gentle anatomy to companioning. Sometimes we use every part of it, other times we simply offer receptive silence and end with a virtues acknowledgment. These are the elements:

1. Open the door with open-ended questions such as "How is

this going?" "What's this like for you?" "What kind of a day are you having?" "Tell me about it."

2. Offer Receptive Silence, if the person is talking freely, so that they can tell you the whole story. The quality of your attention is directly proportional to the degree of your concentration.

3. Ask Cup-Emptying Questions in response to the individual's words. "What" or "how" are the key words. If you ask, "How is this for you?" and he says, "Terrible", you ask "What's terrible?" If she says, "I was just shocked by the news," and says nothing further, ask, "What was shocking?"

4. Focus on physical cues. If the person is holding his hand over his heart, ask "How is your heart?" If he is crying, ask, "What are those tears?" This is far more effective than asking "Why are you crying?", a question that puts people on the defensive or asks them to analyze their feelings. Asking "What's wrong?" judges their tears.

5. Get to the Heart of the Matter sometimes just by silent listening, and sometimes with questions, such as "How has the news affected you?" "What's this like for you?" "What is the hardest part of this?" During one of our sacred mornings, when I asked John, "What is your deepest feeling today?" he said, "Today, there is a wall of tears." After a silence, I asked "What's behind that wall?" He said, "Tears for everything I have had in my life, and for what I haven't had." He leaned his head back and wept. Of course, I joined him.

6. Ask Virtues Reflection Questions. When the person seems to have emptied his cup and gotten to the heart of the matter, it is often useful to ask questions that help him to reflect on the virtue he needs to call on. "What would give you peace about this?" "What will help you to get through

this?" "What does this mean to you?" Or simply, "What do you need?" to invite truthfulness. This is NOT a time to offer advice. Let him discover his own wisdom, not yours.

7. Ask Closure and Integration Questions. Asking positive questions at the end of any conversation, especially companioning, allows the individual to integrate meaning. "What's been helpful about talking today?" "What's been meaningful for you this morning?" "What did you appreciate most about our talk?" Then share what you appreciate as well. When I asked John that question, he said, "I feel I can take an honest look and say anything, anything at all."

8. Give a Virtues Acknowledgment. I believe in closing just about any conversation with a virtue, and particularly when someone has been vulnerable and allowed me to companion them. The more specific the virtue is to what they have shared, the better. When John spoke of his wall of tears, I recall saying, "John, you are being so truthful about your life… and I see your gratitude for the gifts you have had." His face lit up in a huge smile.

III WHAT HELPS & WHAT DOESN'T

"Don't do unto others as you would have them do unto you.
They may have different tastes."
George Bernard Shaw, Irish playwright

What do you do when someone you love has just learned they are going to die? What do you say to a friend who is grief-stricken? What are the taboos to avoid so as not to make it worse?

In the presence of a dying person or one who is bereft and grieving, many people feel inept. They don't know what to say or do and so they often err on the side of doing nothing, or uttering little reassurances that somehow make it worse, not better.

We all need to be aware of how to help one another through these inevitable experiences of loss and death. For this reason, I want to share both as a hospice professional and from my own personal journey what helps and what doesn't.

11 HELP STRIKES AGAIN:
The Seven Deadly Sins of the Well-Meaning

*"Please call me by my true names; so I can hear all my cries and
laughs at once, so I can see that my joy and pain are one."*
Thich Nhat Hanh, Tibetan Buddhist monk

People mean well. Yet, sometimes the way we act around dying
people or those stricken by grief and loss makes things worse, not
better. We bring cold comfort.

John was popular. He had many close friends, and as one of the
three founders of The Virtues Project, he was also loved and
admired by our global network of Virtues Project facilitators. He
received cards, calls, visits, offers from near strangers to move
in with him and help take care of him, and emails galore. Some
brought a balm of compassion. Others were merely annoying, some
disruptive, and some created needless anxiety. I found that I had to
become a diligent gatekeeper according to John's wishes.

Meanwhile, the responses I received as one already feeling bereft
with anticipatory grief, varied from deeply helpful to what I
experienced as bullying. Some offered a soft place to land and
others, despite the best intentions, ran roughshod over my heart.
Here are some of the errors people commit in trying to be helpful.

Seven Sins of the Well-Meaning

1.Taking Over/Overtaking

Everyone who receives the news that death is imminent takes it
personally, each in his or her own way. There is a full gamut of
emotions and no way to predict what the individual's response
is going to be. For this reason, it is deeply disrespectful to jump
to a solution or assume an attitude before learning what that
person is feeling. Saying to the recently diagnosed, "We'll fight
this! What does that doctor know? We'll get a second opinion,"

The mother of a twelve-year-old with brain cancer, who was a deeply religious Christian, told me she finally stopped her well-meaning church family from bringing miracle cure after cure, in the form of special rituals, intensive prayer sessions, and healing waters. Her son was becoming exhausted from it all. "Now I only let a few people visit, who I know will sit with us, make him laugh, or just be there."

There are respectful and palatable ways to offer ideas for hope and healing. An acquaintance in our local community was traveling to Brazil to see John of God, known for healing the sick. She called one day and asked very courteously, "Would John like me to bring his photo there?" John was actually quite enthused about this idea, not as a reversal of his diagnosis necessarily, but the thought of prayer of any kind cheered his heart.

Then there are friends who sincerely believe they know what's best, and you don't. A woman whose husband was dying told me that she became annoyed by friends who would say, "You should take time for yourself. You need a break", when all she wanted was to be with her husband until he died. Better for them to ask what she needed. My friend, Lee, said that after her husband Sam died, her friends refused to leave her alone. All she wanted was the solitude to write in her journal, to sort out her feelings, to explore and unravel what had happened. This forced companionship prolonged her confusion. She needed to find her own pathway through grief.

4. Giving Too Much or Too Little Touch

We cannot assume anything about a dying person, including whether they want us to hold their hands, stroke their brows or massage their feet. Nor can we know for sure if they don't want touch at a given time. We need to follow their cues. I have learned in my healing work with traumatized individuals that sometimes a hug cuts them off from expressing tears. Others need the comfort of an embrace to let the tears flow. For myself, I find that when someone grabs me as soon as they see the tears begin, they are asking me to stop crying. But if they wait, and sense that I need a hug, I experience the hug as permission.

At a First Nations conference where I was a speaker, someone ran up to me and asked me to come to a private room, where members of a community were gathering. They had just learned of a tragic multi-car accident that had killed several generations of people in their large extended family. I remember during the healing circle, feeling moved to kneel before a dry-eyed elder. I opened my arms, and she fell against me, finally able to weep.

Intimacy that is not welcome will soon be apparent. The person will flinch away, or stiffen up. If it is wanted, they will respond. Offer, don't impose.

5. Ignoring

When a caregiver is tending to a beloved companion who is dying, and others try to engage them on the same level they're used to, it doesn't work. They are in a different world now. So, a call to talk about a committee issue can seem deeply insensitive. As my friend Jackie said, "Your priorities are totally changed." I stepped away completely from the hundreds of weekly emails, calls, and requests I normally dealt with as a founder of The Virtues Project so that I could fully concentrate on John's needs. Lo and behold, the world didn't end. Others stepped in. I once heard another speaker at a women's conference on leadership say, "When you make a hole, others will fill it."

After John died, I found it particularly painful when people said nothing – as if nothing had changed, when everything had changed. How could they ignore the gaping hole in my world? This was a painful denial of my reality.

Doing or saying nothing, carrying on as if that will banish the pain of loss is like watching the Titanic sink, the water closing over it, as if it had never been there. Then pretending nothing had happened. A hapless woman called me shortly after my father's death, and asked me to serve on some committee. She said nothing about my loss. I said, "Aren't you going to say anything? I just lost my father." The poor woman said, "I don't know what to say." "Just 'I'm sorry' is enough", I told her, "I'm sorry for your loss."

The grief my eighty-five year old mother in law experienced after losing two of her children to cancer within a few weeks was compounded by the fact that the calls and cards stopped shortly afterward. "You need to hear from people when the grief hits you," she said.

Sometimes people ignore a grieving person's feelings by making assumptions. A woman whose husband died suddenly in a farm accident, was left to manage a full working farm and to parent her three young children on her own. A neighbour thoughtlessly asked her, "What will you do with all the extra time you have now that Jim is gone?" It would be more helpful (and far more tactful!) to ask, "How has life changed for you since Jim's death?"

6. Rationalizing/Reassuring

After a loss, many people rush the grieving person, out of a desire to comfort them, I'm sure. When people told me, "You'll be fine after a year", or "You'll have even more joy after this", or "This will give you many gifts", most of the time it felt invalidating. "But that isn't where I am now!" I felt like shouting, as I smiled and nodded. One time it was helpful. I went to my grief therapist, Dr. Tom Gilligan, and bawled my eyes out, as he companioned me patiently. I said, "I feel like I'll never be myself again." He said, "You're right. You won't." He paused and said, "You'll be better." Somehow, the timing was right. And I had had plenty of time in the session to empty my cup first. I think that is the key. When one's cup is full, trying to put something in it just results in it spilling out. Most of the time, it is best to simply meet the grieving person right where they are at that moment, trusting that their journey is unfolding as it should.

Many people believe they have to offer little sayings that supposedly make sense of death and loss. Too often, they merely minimize and invalidate the person's experience. "God wanted him more than we needed him." Really? How about a different interpretation that doesn't paint the almighty as a self-serving sadist? John believed that everything that happens is for our learning, that Grace takes many forms. And did he ever learn! One time I heard about art therapy for the dying, and asked him, "Does that interest you?" He said, "I've been a designer all my life. Now the only art that interests me is the Divine art of living."

I gave a workshop once called "Good Grief". I asked each person in the group to share what was helpful and what was not. A young woman who had lost her husband, two decades her senior, was grieving deeply. She said that what hurt and angered her most was the frequent statement people made to her, "You're young. You'll marry again." This so backfired from its intention to bring her hope. It invalidated her deep love for her husband by projecting a future which she was in no way prepared to contemplate.

When an elderly parent dies, even when this individual was a lifeline to an adult child left behind, saying, "Well, she lived a good long life," does nothing but belittle the pain of the individual and add a soupcon of guilt to her feelings of loss.

7. Prolonging Death

We have a death-denying culture, both in western society at large, and in our medical system. Too often, a terminally or chronically ill person, when they have a medical crisis, ends up in expensive torment in the Intensive Care Unit of a hospital. Unless there is active intervention by the family and the willing participation of their physician to move the individual into palliative care, every effort will be made to just keep them breathing. The resistance to death as a natural process that should be surrounded by comfort and peace often causes needless pain and very pricey misery for everyone concerned.

My friend, Jackie's husband Doug was dying of Glio Blastoma Multiform at the same time as John. She said that when unusual symptoms would arise, such as a blood clot in Doug's leg, she said to him, "Sweetheart, this is serious. What do you want me to do? Call 911? Do you want to go to Emergency?" "No, I'd rather die at home in your arms," he said. And she calmly accepted his decision, realizing this could be his chosen end. Other people finding out about it would look totally shocked or say, "Why didn't you call for an ambulance?" or "Don't you need to get him to the hospital?" These decisions are personal, and the only remaining expression of independence the dying person has. To force anything on them, including food, when they no longer want it, is a violation of their most fragile and sacred boundaries.

With all due respect, physicians and other medical professionals are honour bound to do whatever is necessary to preserve life. Heroic efforts, which often occur in the absence of a Do Not Resuscitate form signed when the dying individual is capable of rational thought, do not prolong life. They prolong death. This is no kindness to anyone. The kindest doctors know when it is time to call in hospice.

"False optimism is like administering stimulants to an exhausted nervous system."
Sam Keen, American author & philosopher

SUSTAINING VIRTUES:

Empathy is the ability to put ourselves in another's place and to understand their experience. We are deeply present to their thoughts and feelings with such compassionate accuracy that they can hear their own thoughts more clearly.

Tact is telling the truth kindly. We think before we speak, aware of how deeply our words affect others. When our words are weighty, we weigh our words, knowing they have the power to cause pain or to uplift. Tact helps us to discern what to say and what is better left unsaid. Tact is good timing. It is the diplomacy of the heart.

HEALING STEPS:

1. Never assume you know what someone needs or feels. Ask. Listen. Patiently observe. Be present. When death is imminent, offer care, not cure. Meet them where they are with gentle curiosity, not manufactured sympathy or automatic rescue efforts.

2. If you know of a remedy that can help, even a miracle cure, ask them respectfully if they are interested. If you get a whiff of resistance, back off. This is their life.

3. Remember to stay in touch with grieving people. Their grief doesn't heal quickly. After a death, call the grieving person and then call them six weeks later, when the loss begins to really hit home. Keep connecting. My friend Ellen, whom I hadn't seen in the six months since John died, met me and Dan at the airport, looked into my eyes and said "How are you, Linda… with John?" I so appreciated her understanding that grief takes time and that I was still in need of companioning.

allowing entry into private grieving and dawning insights.

Check In Regularly

Story keepers who check in often to ask a caregiver, "How are things today?" and are willing to hear the details, bring sweet relief. And the fact that they can easily pick up the thread of the ongoing story makes it easier to talk with them.

John's next door neighbour, Jennifer, called me several times a week just to listen. Having an interested listener outside the family, who was more detached, was a Godsend for me. When a friend or acquaintance is facing loss, I say to them, "If you ever need to talk to someone not so close to home, please feel free to call me." And then I call them.

Strangely, when someone offered to companion me, I usually said no. But when they just did it naturally by asking, "How are you, really, Linda?" or "What's going on?" "How are things today?" I would immediately respond. Those calls helped immeasurably.

Act with Tact

It is also helpful to know when to remain silent and not say anything. Just be there. Sometimes a dying person is experiencing a period of relief through denial. Let them be. Don't initiate talk of death unless they do.

Accept Respite Time

Caregivers need breaks. We need to accept offers from friends willing to drive or garden or pick up groceries, or spend time with the one we are caring for. There are home care workers we can hire to come in and do simple chores or take the night shift.

Call on Your Palliative Care Team

Palliative care teams, often connected with a local hospice, include visiting nurses, who are warm, helpful and honest. They were a great support to John and me.

The brain surgeon told me John was developing severe osteoporosis from the steroid medication he was taking. He said, "Whatever you do, don't let him fall!" It can be terrifying to believe that a loved one's wellbeing and safety is in your hands. I felt totally responsible, and literally caught John three times to prevent a fall.

The day he wanted to give up his walker and walk on his own, I panicked, and called the palliative care nurse, Sharon. She said, "Linda, if he falls, he falls. It's his life. If he wants to stop using the walker, let him. Even if he breaks a hip, it doesn't matter. He will die one way or another." Our primary care doctor told me not to worry, and to let John go out with other people. "It doesn't matter now. Whatever happens, even if you're not with him, it's fine. You can`t protect him." This took a weight off me. It brought home the fact that I was not in control and I couldn`t stop the course of John's death. It was a relief to be reminded that it wasn`t in my power.

When John had his final seizure, he was taken to the palliative care suite at our local hospital overnight. I stayed with him. Nurse Sharon called me when she found out, and told me, "It might get ugly." And it did. Just having that honest warning helped me to prepare myself.

Be Yourself
Dying people and their caregivers don't want to be around dour, maudlin people. Just treat them normally. Meet them where they are. If they are having a tearful day, know that those are healing tears, and just be there with quiet empathy. If you have a joking relationship with the individual, this is no time to stop. It honors them to recognize that they are still whole, still themselves. If they were very social during their normal lives, they will continue to want visitors. If they were loners, this is not likely to change when they are dying.

Cards and Notes Help
We had a friend named Lynda, one of our virtues facilitators, who sent cards once or twice a week. They ranged from funny to

brought him great comfort. Almost everyone loves a soothing hand or foot rub.

Keepsakes

Going through photo albums stirs memories and creates the opening for life stories. Tamara, a creative woman who owned a bed and breakfast on a remote island, made a collage of photos for a guest after her husband died. The couple had visited her bed and breakfast several times. As a professional photographer, she had taken many photos of them on her boat, climbing hills, enjoying tea together. What a precious gift it was months after her guest had lost her husband.

Furry Friends

Animals are therapeutic. When they are brought into a hospice or hospital, they leave a trail of lightened hearts and tender smiles. A cherished pet can give deep comfort to a dying or grieving person. John's beautiful cat, Misha, a silky silver black and white American short hair, rarely left his lap once he was diagnosed. The cuddling was a balm to them both. He would hold her and stroke her for hours and then they would both fall asleep. If he went into the bathroom, she would literally stand on her hind legs and bang on the door until he came out. Misha somehow knew when John died. She howled for three days.

Outings

Just as we all need a break from our normal surroundings, whenever a dying person or a grieving caregiver can get out for some time away from the normal routine, it literally gives them a breath of fresh air. One of the gifts I give to close friends who are caregiving is a "spa-ahh" day. I companion them over a lovely meal somewhere special, then we soak and get massages or pedicures. Of course John, as an inveterate lunchist, enjoyed going to different restaurants and art galleries with friends. He did this as long as he was at all mobile, including two days before he died, when we took him to our home for a fried chicken dinner with all the trimmings.

Beauty

Beauty nurtures the soul. We are blessed to live on an island in British Columbia, one of the most beautiful spots on earth. John soaked in the view from his dining room windows, of ocean and mountains in the distance. He had never looked at it with such depth of awareness and appreciation before. He would gaze at the changing light on the golden wood walls of his living room and say, "I love this house. It's so beautiful."

My friend Jackie's husband Doug, said to her as he was dying, "There's such beauty in every moment." Mary, one of the women I companioned at Hospice years before had said to me, "People feel sorry for old people. But they don't know." "What don't they know, Mary?" I asked. "The beauty. The beauty of words." Mary was a writer, who had hidden her exquisite stories away until I asked to see them.

One of my companioning buddies was Judy, a filmmaker whose adored partner Neil had just died of brain cancer around the time that John did. One day Judy showed me his art and the last paintings he made. They were covered with words. She said, "He would splash and spill, and the paint would be all over his clothes. He painted with such passion." Judi granted me the privilege of quoting here some of the words Neil had hand painted across his colorful canvasses:

Being fully present with God. A formless God. A giving God. Full spectrum. Emanating light, colour, warmth, kindness, joy, laughter and fun. Chromatic. Harmonic. Perceiving. All knowing. All understanding.

And another that reflected the same wild joy John had expressed: SEIZE THE MOMENT! Grab the brushes, the pens, or whatever and JUST DO IT! LET GO OF ALL FEAR and LET WHAT WILL BE. The DIVINE will guide your every move and bring them all together to make a HARMONIOUS whole! You'll be AMAZED! None of your work will ever be the same again! A real TRANSFORMATION!

The gift of beauty – in words, in paint, in dance, music or sculpture – is twice blessed. It blesses those who create it, and those of us who have the honor to witness it.

> *"The human soul needs actual beauty more than bread."*
> D.H. Lawrence, author

SUSTAINING VIRTUES:

Creativity connects us to beauty of sound, design, color, movement, ideas and words, and allows us to bring something original into the world. It is a portal to inspiration.

Beauty is a sense of wonder and reverence for the harmony, color, and loveliness of the world. Beauty opens us to the deep patterns of life that inform and delight us. It nurtures our souls.

HEALING STEPS:

1. Take the time for outings. Change refreshes all of us.

2. Be mindful that animals can bring a healing presence.

3. Be creative in providing simple comforts and inspiring moments for those who are dying and for yourself as a caregiver.

14 A FEW LAUGHS

"It's not that I'm afraid of death.
I just don't want to be there when it happens."
Woody Allen, comedian & filmmaker

John developed a whole new genre of humor that buoyed everyone around him throughout his last months. Much of it was what some would call "gallows humor", surrounding the touchy issue of death with laughter. For example, he would say, with exaggerated emphasis, "I`m just dying to try that new restaurant." One time, with a completely straight face, he said, "The palliative care on this island is to die for." After the briefest pause, we both burst out laughing.

He and I inherited my mother's huge belly laugh, loud enough to turn heads. One time years ago, John had gone off to Victoria to visit friends for several days. I went in for the day to go to a movie. At the first funny bit, I laughed and heard an echoing guffaw from across the darkened theater. "John?" I called out. "Lin?" he said. We laughed long and loud together every day before he died. And even after.

Author and editor of The Saturday Review, Norman Cousins wrote Anatomy of an Illness, the story of how he literally laughed his way back to health after being diagnosed with a rare, life-threatening illness. While in the hospital, Cousins hypothesized that if negative emotions such as anger and frustration could contribute to poor health, why couldn't positive emotions such as joy and laughter have the opposite effect? He left the hospital to stay in a hotel room (likely a much more sterile environment), took large quantities of Vitamin C, had a projector brought in, and watched Marx Brothers movies and episodes of Candid Camera. He laughed heartily every day. Within a few weeks he was back to work at the Saturday Review, and although he still had some minor physical difficulties, his body continued to recover as he sustained his self-directed wellness program. It is now well recognized that laughter boosts the immune system.

As I have described earlier, John never stopped delivering his typical one-liners, such as the first time he emerged from the radiation chamber holding his radiation mask in his hand, saying, "Those fencing lessons aren't what they're cracked up to be." Another day we were going downtown and a deer trotted out onto the road. Without missing a beat, John said, "Hello, deah!" in a thick New York accent.

I was cleaning out his typically over-stocked fridge one morning and said, "John, do you really use all these exotic condiments?" He said, "You know what they say. Eat safely. Use a condiment."

Years ago, Dan and I visited a friend and his wife, who was dying. He seemed buoyant, even jolly about it and said his wife was dealing with it all with great humor and acceptance. "Just ask her how she is. She loves to give this answer she's come up with." So, when we went into her room at hospice, we did. "Progressing nicely," she said, a big grin illuminating her pale face.

A friend's father who had terminal cancer was known for his fabulous sense of humour, and it did not desert him in his final months. He was a bit frustrated by friends who started avoiding him or treating him differently. He said to his son, "The next time one of the neighbors comes by with a long face, I'm going to lie on the floor holding a lily. Open the door wide and tell them, 'You just missed him.'"

My son, Chris asked me to take his friend, poet Roger White, to dinner on his behalf as I could get to Vancouver much more easily than Chris could from Australia, where he was living. Roger was in the final stages of cancer. Chris's instructions were "No vegetables and make sure there's chocolate." After initial small talk, I asked Roger, "How are you really?" He smiled and said, "Well, I'm not buying any green bananas." We both laughed so loud, there was a sudden silence in this rather fancy restaurant.

John's humor never let up, even the night before he died. After a last dramatic seizure, he spent his last night in the palliative care suite of our local hospital. He went in and out of coma. Some friends came to see him and asked how he was. I mentioned that he hadn't eaten all day. Our friend Louise joked "And I was going to make you a blueberry pie." In a garbled but unmistakeable voice, John responded, "WAS?!!!"

I personally believe that John's optimism and humor (and to some extent my cooking) extended his life by many months.

"Laughter is the best medicine."
Author unknown

SUSTAINING VIRTUES:

Authenticity – Being genuine, letting your true self shine through. Being real in the presence of death gives permission to others to do the same.

Humor – An aspect of the virtues of joy and enthusiasm, humor is a catalyst for acceptance. It bonds us in our experience of being human.

HEALING STEPS:

1. Be yourself in the presence of someone who is dying. Sooner or later, we will all be there. We need the comfort of being able to be real together.

2. Let humor carry you through the journey of loss. It provides great comic relief.

IV CARE FOR THE CAREGIVER

"If our compassion does not include ourselves, it is incomplete."
Jack Kornfield, Buddhist teacher & author

Neglecting self-care is an occupational hazard for many caregivers.
We are so focused on a loved one's care that we take no time or
space to sustain our own health. Caregivers have been known to
collapse and even die first unless they have regular ways to rest,
restore, and revive themselves.

How do we summon the detachment to ask ourselves what we
need? How can we tell when it's time to bring in supplementary
care, or even move the dying person to a professional care facility
or hospice?

How can we survive and even thrive through the roller coaster of
emotions we experience in caring for another soul? What practices
can sustain us not only while we are tending our loved one until
they die, but afterwards in our bereavement?

15 COMPASSION FATIGUE

*"Caregiving is a marathon, not a sprint, and requires a healthy
lifestyle for the body, mind and spirit."*
www.abta.org

Like other caregivers tending someone they love deeply, I was
utterly dedicated to John's wellbeing as he was dying. I became
totally immersed in his care. It was as if I were melding with him,
just as I had with my children when they were babies. An invisible
force field encapsulated us, merging us into one entity. In the last
months, it was an effort to focus on anyone else, even my husband,
Dan. Everyone and everything else felt like a distraction. Co-
dependence be damned! There was nothing that could move me
from this single-pointed concentration on John's comfort and care.

The Dangers of Selflessness

It is not uncommon for caregivers to identify so intensely with the
role they are playing, that all other relationships and roles become
dim shadows merely lingering outside their field of attention.

I was acutely aware of the slightest change in John's symptoms,
his moods, and his stability. His needs became my skills. I had
become his cook, his minder, his constant spiritual companion,
and perhaps most importantly, his drug czarina. I became an
expert at monitoring and dispensing his medications, which at first
I had been barely able to pronounce. During one of our sacred
mornings, he said, "Linda, today I have a new virtue for you –
Sensei. You are a master at knowing my needs."

The biggest danger in losing oneself in the role of caregiving is
that we easily slip into the habit of neglecting ourselves, physically,
mentally, emotionally, and spiritually. As self-care deteriorates, so
does our ability to be effective in caring for another. We often end
up on a roller coaster of emotion, from empathy to resentment to
anger to helplessness and anxiety.

"When it is dark enough, you can see the stars."
Ralph Waldo Emerson, American philosopher

SUSTAINING VIRTUES:

Humility – We willingly serve others and accept help when we need it. We don't try to do it all ourselves. Martyring ourselves becomes a spiritual assault on the one we are caring for. We give our very best, and trust that it is enough. We know we are resilient, not perfect.

Wisdom is the guardian of our choices. It helps us to discern the right path at the right moment. It gives us clarity of thought and deeper understanding. We use our best judgment, resisting the pull of impulse and desire. Wisdom gives us the maturity and patience to make sustainable decisions. Caregivers need to call on wisdom sooner rather than later.

HEALING STEPS:

1. Be aware that there is a limit to self-sacrifice, not only for your sake but for the sake of the one you are caring for.

2. Have the humility and wisdom to seek help before you cause damage to yourself, physically or emotionally.

3. Trust the fact that you are not in control. You can contribute. You can help. But you cannot do it all.

16 VITAMIN T

"Those who wait on the Lord shall renew their strength.
They shall mount up on wings as eagles.
They shall run and not be weary; they shall walk and not faint."
Isaiah 40

I am in awe of the level of trust and acceptance I have witnessed in so many dying people, John most of all. He was a radiant example to everyone who met him.

Surprising Graces

The seed of courageous surrender began early after John's diagnosis. After his initial seizures signalling the presence of a brain tumor, he was told he couldn't drive for a year and only then if he remained seizure free. At the same time, he was told he probably would not live for more than three months. For John, driving went beyond independence and freedom. It was one of his joys. He pored over his monthly Car & Driver magazines as if they were juicy novels. He spoke the "language of car" with Dan and other aficionados. He adorned his silver Audi with every bell and whistle available. That car was like an extension of his body, a primal expression of his fierce enthusiasm. He loved to whip along, veering around corners, but expertly, without a wasted inch. He was a devotee of speed.

When we were children, our brother Tommy and I used to tease him about falling up the stairs. He ran upstairs so fast, he would usually trip once or twice. We called him "Mr. Toad" after the beloved character in Kenneth Grahame's Wind in the Willows, which my mother read aloud to us at bedtime. Like John, Mr. Toad was addicted to "motor cars". Whenever he saw one, his eyes swirled around crazily. When John had the opportunity to design Mr. Toad's Wild Ride at Disneyland, we saw it as perfect synchronicity.

When John was forbidden to drive, I was awed by his acceptance, acquiescing so serenely to the loss of one of his deepest pleasures.

shouted back, "It's not easy for me to trust when you're in pain!" John, in classic companioning mode, asked me, "What makes it hard for you to trust when I'm in pain?" I began to cry, and said, "I guess I feel as though God is abandoning you." He smiled gently and said, "But it's not true. Even in the midst of the pain, I feel the hand of God."

Be Peaceful with What Is

This revelation somehow helped me to downshift into a gentle detachment. It supported me to face John's increasing days of breakthrough pain calmly, even trustingly, knowing we would get through this, and that John would be released soon, and free of all pain.

At the recommendation of the emergency room physician, I also made my first appointment to see a local psychologist who specialized in grief and death. He told me something powerfully freeing. "Do you know that there is a difference between pain and suffering? John has the pain but you have the suffering." When I went home and shared this with John, he smiled sweetly and said, "Bingo! You and your damn empathy. I can't even remember the seizures, but you remember it all."

Since John's death, I have sensed his presence and heard his voice several times, when I most needed comfort, reminding me, "Vitamin T, Lin, vitamin T", bringing me a fresh breath of trust, giving me peace.

"All I have seen teaches me to trust the Creator for all I have not seen."
    Ralph Waldo Emerson, American poet

SUSTAINING VIRTUES:

Trust is being sure, in the depths of our being, that there is some gift or learning in everything that happens. We move confidently with the flow of life, gathering strength from adversity. We know we are never alone. Trust is leaning into what is.

Detachment is experiencing our feelings without allowing them to control us. We step back and look at things objectively. We let go and accept what we cannot change with courage and acceptance.

HEALING STEPS:

1. Ask yourself what you need, to be as peaceful as possible during the ordeals of loss, whether you are facing your own death or serving as caregiver.

2. GET HELP! If you are in the role of caregiver, don't wait too long to get supplementary or relief help.

3. Contact hospice sooner rather than later, if the dying person is open to it. In most communities there are hospices that offer or can refer you to a range of resources you need, from home care nurses to volunteers to professional grief counsellors. Don't wait until the last phase of terminal illness. As soon as a diagnosis is made, hospice has ways to help. Calling them does not mean giving up. It is reaching out to improve quality of life for everyone involved.

17 SURVIVAL STRATEGIES

"I'd like to make a motion that we face reality."
Bob Newhart, television show

John's continual choice to face death in a positive way helped him negotiate all the twists and turns, the losses and changes as the end of life approached. As the caregiver, I also had many choice points. Sometimes, as I have explained, I took self-sacrifice too far, as many do. Yet, I had many teachable moments along the way in learning how to survive a traumatic, inconceivable loss.

Proactive Practices

First and foremost, a caregiver needs to keep his or her self-care cup full. If we are running on empty, we have nothing left to give. Here is a list of basic habits one needs to cultivate in the midst of loss and grief. Whether you are mourning a sudden death, or are caring for your loved one for months or years, these simple practices will sustain you.

1. Keep Your Body Nourished

First and foremost, take care to drink a good deal of water. Keep yourself hydrated at all times. Avoid sweet drinks that raise your blood sugar, then cause it to drop an hour later. Eat nutritious meals and snacks, including lots of fruit, veggies, and grains. Keep your protein intake up with eggs, cheese, meat, nuts and legumes. Take the time to make or get enjoyable meals, even when your loved one is not eating much. Keep good chocolate around and administer with moderation.

2. Take the time each day for moderate exercise

Find a way to walk, swim, run, or do yoga, if only in your chair. I used my Nordic poles to walk for 15 minutes most mornings and found it refreshed me for the long days of caregiving, cooking and companioning.

3. Rest Proactively

This means to lie down once a day before you get tired. This practice was a Godsend for me and a really major part of what sustained me. Even if you just sit back in a comfortable chair supporting your back and neck and watch television or read something engaging for an hour, truly resting your mind and body, this will make all the difference.

4. Get enough sleep

If you cannot sleep, ask your doctor or homeopath for something mild to help. Our palliative care nurses recommended Gravol or what is called Dramamine in the U.S., containing dimenhydrinate. Advil PM contains it too. There are rarely side-effects and it allows one to relax enough to sleep. Any homeopathic remedy including tryptophan can help as well. John took something stronger prescribed by his doctor, and it helped him sleep well throughout his illness.

5. Make time to play

Spend time with people and activities you enjoy. Go to a movie. Have a spa day. Go out for lunch with a friend. Play a round of golf. It will do wonders in giving you some balance, a regular respite from responsibility.

6. Get respite help

Whether calling on friends, family, or a professional home care worker, have someone regularly take over the caregiving role. At one point, Dan insisted that I go back to our house to rest each afternoon, purposefully out of range of my "John radar". John and I both needed others to come and help. So, I happily became John's social secretary. I asked him to make a list of friends with whom he wanted to spend time. They eagerly agreed to come to the house or take him for an outing. When our wonderful home care worker came once a week, I was completely at peace, trusting that she knew what to do.

7. Have a regular Routine of Reverence

Find a way to spend a few moments each day in reflection, prayer or meditation. There are many ways to do it. There is walking meditation, prayer journaling, visual meditation where you picture going to a place of beauty, seeking guidance or simply peace, chanting, the practice of silence and breath. Any of these can powerfully revive you.

8. Keep a Grief Journal

Even before your loved one dies, it is helpful to name what you are feeling and experiencing. Writing about it with total honesty as if to a really good friend gives you private freedom to empty your cup. Mine is a prayer journal and I write to God, as the great friend and companion.

9. Talk to a Counselor

Have regular talks with a hospice volunteer, a professional grief counselor or both. You need a safe place to empty your cup of tears, anger or fear, or whatever you are feeling, with someone objective who knows how to companion without judging.

10. Take Daycations

Getting away for even one day to the home of a friend, for a game of golf or tennis, or a night at a retreat center is a marvellous way to recharge. Personal care treatments such as massage or Reiki revive us so that we have more to give.

For over a year, I had been booked to speak at Queenswood, a nearby spiritual retreat centre, as part of their "Passionate Lives" dinner and lecture series. I stepped away from my constant responsibilities as caregiver for exactly 24 hours, and entered another world. I enjoyed every moment of it! I went early so I could nap, pray, walk on the beach, and prepare. I enjoyed sparkling conversation at the dinner table, then went into the chapel, which was packed with more than 200 people. I shared the adventures and blessings Dan, John and I had experienced for more than two decades as founders of The Virtues Project.

I dedicated the talk to John, and ended with a prayer for him. When I finished, there was thunderous applause. There were many tears and laughs during the talk, and I returned home deeply renewed, ready for the last intense week of John's life.

11. Plan LFTs (Look Forward To's)

When we are losing a loved one, and especially if we are the primary caregiver, we need LFTs – plans to look forward to after the death occurs. It sustains our hope, and reminds us that life will go on, and that we will experience joy again.

Dan and I planned a trip in December to the Cook Islands in the South Pacific, a place of tranquil beauty where we had gone before. The thought of lying in the sun, a breeze blowing through palm fronds overhead, snorkelling in crystal clear water, got us through the hardest hours. I called it my "spabattical" and planned to indulge in as many massages as I wanted.

We chose to go nearly six months after John's passing, knowing we would need time to sort his estate and were able to finish almost everything before we left. Every evening at the little boutique resort, the staff would ask us what we had done that day. We would look at each other, smile, and say "Absolutely nothing." I spent hours reading in a hammock beneath a swaying palm, napping, and swimming in the ocean a few steps from our bungalow deck. I spent time each morning writing *Graceful Endings*. It often brought me to tears, which was very healing.

My friend, Jackie, who had sailed the world with her husband, Doug, took a trip on a sailing ship six weeks after he died. Being at sea again, with all responsibilities looked after, being served lovely meals, and having people to be with or not, as she chose, was deeply restorative for her. She took along a sketch book and would sit quietly on deck for hours, sometimes just holding it. This was a signal to other guests to respect her privacy.

circle with other residents, to talk about their experience of cancer.
They also did Virtues Picks using the Virtues Reflection Cards,
each person randomly picking a card after sharing their story. One
evening John raised the question, "How do you think of your cancer?
How would you describe it?" Each one in turn called it "a gift."

In the weeks and months to come, this came to mean even more
to John, as he found himself entering a new inner realm. His
understanding of ideas became more acute, his appreciation for
ordinary pleasures deepened, he was more intensely engaged in
an awareness of faith and wonder, and his sense of beauty and joy
expanded as never before. He found life literally awesome. This is
not an unusual attitude amongst the dying. There is often a new
radiance that comes over them as death approaches.

Shortly after John returned home from the Cancer Lodge, he had
a visit from Morley Myers, a long-time friend and well-known
Canadian sculptor. Hearing of John's attitude that this illness was
an intriguing adventure, Morley decided to gift John with one of
his pieces. It was entitled "Ram's Head", as an homage to a work
by Picasso. John asked Morley to mount it in the dining room
between two large windows with the view of mountains and ocean
he enjoyed each day. John adored that piece. One day, he sat
silently taking in its rugged beauty, and said, "That sculpture is very
meaningful to me. It reminds me of how I feel – as if I have come
out of all of life's pressures and chaos, and am somehow emerging."
I said, "It's as if you refuse to consider this an emergency. Instead
it's your emergence." A big smile lit up his face. "Yes! I'm going to
call it 'Emergence.'" With Morley's heartfelt permission, Dan and
I fulfilled one of John's last wishes by designing his gravestone to
incorporate that sculpture. Many months later, on the day the
granite slab with the "Emergence" sculpture was being laid on
John's grave, Morley "happened" to be cycling past the cemetery,
and the man who was laying the gravestone beckoned him to stop.
Morley helped to place it with his own hands.

Unconditional Prayer
One morning, during our sacred time, John was musing about prayer. He said, "It has really changed for me." "How?" I asked. "Well, I used to pray every day, as a duty. Now it's totally different." "What is it now?" I asked. "Now it's food. It's my daily nutrition."

Interestingly, the tenor of John's relationship with the Divine was not about petition, which is to ask for what one wants. Often, when someone has a terminal illness, it is natural to ask for healing. John did recite healing prayers at first, but soon, he said, "It doesn't feel right to be asking God for healing. I need something else." What he was drawn to was the simple practice of opening to God's will. And gratitude, constant gratitude, for the grace he had experienced throughout his life – particularly the many opportunities he had received to be of service.

Grace in Life's Lessons
This sense of grace extended to those teachable moments of the soul which come only from the refining fire of tests, the crucible of the ego from which our virtues emerge.

I was reading to John a section of my book, *A Pace of Grace*, entitled "Ask Your Angels", which speaks of the A-Team of ancestors, angels and advisors that I believe each of us has as our spiritual support team in the spiritual realm. He remained silent for several minutes. Then he said, "I learned years ago that my work would be so much better if I simply opened myself to inspiration following purposeful prayer. I'm just so grateful to that Power. There isn't a single project I have ever worked on that didn't include that prayer."

We talked about how the kind of prayer in which we seek guidance is like digging out a channel for the waters of grace. John went on to say, "You know, it's surprising how different the impact can be," referring to when we rely on Divine assistance versus when we practice functional atheism – attempting to do it all on our own, without God. He recounted a time in the early days of working with

19 LAST WISHES

"Once someone has been made aware that their time is limited, their unfulfilled dreams may take on a new importance. 'Someday' has to be right now."
Elizabeth Grace, author

Having advance notice that life is coming to an end has certain advantages. One is that the dying person can reflect on their "bucket list" – the things they want to do or the people they want to see before they die. Last wishes of the terminally ill are likely to be as unique as the individuals themselves, with no two people hoping for exactly the same experience. In the end, what matters most is giving a dying person the chance to express his or her desires. And then offer what is possible. Just having the freedom to articulate a wish brings some satisfaction, albeit often a bittersweet one.

Some last wishes have nothing to do with adventures, but instead are all about things that will bring peace of mind – ending family feuds, getting in touch with long lost loves, and tying up loose ends the individual may be worried about. Some want to plan their own funerals. John wasn't one of those. He gradually became aware of four wishes. They had to do with service, friendship, food, and art.

Soulful Service
John's mobility, mental clarity, and physical stability came and went in waves, depending on the effectiveness of anti-inflammatory medication and the growth of his brain tumor. A month before his second brain surgery, he was mentally foggy, having trouble with words and unable to move without a walker. He looked at me sadly and said, "I feel like a bulb that is dimming." "What's that like for you?" I asked. "It doesn't feel like me. I used to be such a bright light. It's part of my self-image. I have no control over it. And I feel guilty." When I asked what he felt guilty about, he said, "My light is dimming. What's my purpose now?" "What a good question", I said. I left it at that, and John became very pensive.

California Dreaming

Over the next few days, he held that question in quiet discernment. I respected his silence, sensing he was in a deep place. Then at dinner one night, he said to Dan and me, "You know what I wish? I wish I could speak again in Pasadena." He had lived there in the years he worked with Walt Disney Imagineering, and had often spoken on the Baha'i Faith at a "fireside" gathering held in the beautiful home of friends, Judges Jim and Dorothy Nelson. It was a huge part of his life's purpose to serve his faith in this way. There was also a family wedding in Laguna Beach happening soon, and John wanted to meet his twin Tommy there.

True to form, Dan said, "Then, go to California." I rolled my eyes at him in horror, trying to transmit "the glare", thinking, "Are you crazy?" John could barely walk. I had images of wheelchairs, and a seizure on the plane. John said, "Oh, I don't know. That's not very realistic." I breathed a sigh of relief. But Dan kept it up. Each night at dinner, he would say, "I really think you should go." John began to feel hopeful, and a new California wish arose. "I wish I could see my colleagues at Disney and find out what they're doing these days." My last hope was that our doctor would forbid it, knowing John could have a seizure anytime and that we had no medical insurance in the U.S. "Let's ask your doctor," says I, quietly confident she would turn him down.

Our doctor had recently called us to come in for an appointment. She began by saying that the medical team had nothing further to offer John. She seemed on the verge of tears. John simply smiled and said, "Well, I'm content with that. Every day is a gift." Then he added, "What I would like to know is if I can go to California." She looked dumbfounded. To my surprise, she said, "Yes, IF!" and gave instructions that John should remain in a wheelchair at all times. She warned us that the air pressure in the plane could give him a severe headache and added a caveat that if he had a seizure, I should get him home on the next plane. This was terrifying to me, to say the least, but I surrendered to John's excitement and Dan's plan.

A week later, having arranged for wheelchairs to and from the plane, John and I were winging our way to LAX. With a serene smile, John drifted off into a long nap. By the time we arrived, he was refreshed and I had the headache.

Connecting with Old Friends

The day before his talk, John revisited his wish about Disney. He said, "I would so love to visit Disney again." I suggested he call one of his colleagues to see if they could meet for lunch. Joe Lanzisero, a Vice President at Walt Disney Imagineering, was keen to meet with John and arranged lunch for the next day. When he got off the phone, John said he wished he had planned better so he could meet some of the other folks he had worked with on Tokyo Disney. As it turned out, an amazing surprise awaited him at the source of the Magic Kingdom. (More on that in the next chapter.) That day was his sixty-fifth birthday, and he fulfilled his two wishes – to return to WDI and to give a talk.

We were staying in a suite at the glamorous Langham Huntington in Pasadena, restored from its original grandeur as the Langham Grand Hotel of 1865, set on more than twenty lush acres overlooking the immaculate suburbs of San Marino.

The following day, one of John's closest Pasadena buddies, Don, came by in a baby blue Mercedes convertible to take him out for the day. After packing the walker into his trunk, and showing him how to hold John's arm so he wouldn't fall, I headed straight for the spa. John was still energized, but I was exhausted.

Later that evening, Don and two other old friends dropped in with world renowned chocolate bread pudding from a restaurant called Masa. Our suite was spacious enough to accommodate the party, and we all laughed and reminisced.

Our trip ended with a family wedding at sunset on Laguna Beach, where John reunited with other family members, including our brother Tommy.

By the time we boarded the plane for Victoria, John's mobility had improved so much from walking long hotel halls that he no longer needed wheelchair assistance. Dan had put John's favourite CDs on an I-Pod, but John had never used it. He wanted to listen to it on the way home in the plane. I left him to it, respecting his boundary of not wanting my help with technical or electronic things. I prayed, "Please, God, help him." He put in the ear buds, and fiddled a bit with the I-pod.

When I dared to peek over at him, he was staring out the window at the glistening Sierra Nevada Mountains below, tears coursing silently down his cheeks. He turned to me and said, "It doesn't get any better than this. My favourite, Scriabin's "Poem of Ecstasy", is playing. I feel like I'm already in heaven." As he reminisced about this afterwards, I said, "Perhaps this is a foretaste of what's coming." Needless to say, I was deeply grateful that Dan had the foresight to know this trip was possible, and, to be honest, also to myself for finding the courage to make it happen.

Eatathons

To me, preparing food is an expression of love, and I truly enjoy doing it. Fortunately, John loved my cooking, and I made three squares a day, with as much creativity as I could muster, since he was a gourmand who craved variety. Meanwhile, my husband Dan, Mr. Meat and Potatoes, likes the same meal on the same night each week. So, I did my best to nurture both men of the house. However, John would occasionally speak longingly about restaurants in Tokyo and New York. By this time, his slim frame had disappeared in a huge weight gain due to the steroid, Dexamethasone, on which he depended for minimizing brain swelling.

So, the idea arose for an "Eatathon" in nearby Victoria. John and I took the ferry, and stayed at the beautiful Laurel Point Inn in Victoria's inner harbour, where we had held the twentieth anniversary conference for The Virtues Project – the last event John designed. It had a lovely Japanese garden and an excellent restaurant. We arranged to meet friends at as many varied eateries

Ask what they would like to eat. It might be something simple like tapioca pudding that Mom used to make. Take them for a drive. Rearrange their room according to their wishes. Just asking what they wish for is a gift in itself.

20 TRIBUTES & ROASTS

"Now is the time
To give me roses, not to keep them
for my grave to come.
Give them to me while my heart beats,
give them today
while my heart yearns for jubilee.
Now is the time."
Mzwakhe Mbuli, performance artist and activist, South Africa

We tend to honor people after they die. What prevents us from acknowledging them when they are with us? Who wouldn't like to know how we will be remembered, and what our intimates or colleagues love about us? Why not honor each other while we are still here? Offering a living eulogy is the practice of celebrating the life of someone we admire, someone retiring, or someone who is terminally ill.

Crowning Our Elders
Bill Plotkin in his ground-breaking book *Nature and the Human Soul* speaks of the spiritual stages of life, including elderhood. This is a period, he says, when "More and more, you instinctively embody your character in your everyday behaviour..." It is the stage when one moves from doing to being, from accomplishment to celebration, from a task focus to living our values more deeply. Our soul-infused contribution continues in the world, but we allow it rather than push it. John exemplified this shift, from his normal mode of rushing, doing and creating – "Mr. Toad" on steroids – to a radiant, contemplative, quiet being.

Plotkin describes what is needed to mark this passage in life as a "Crowning Ceremony", in which we honor the elder who is emerging into his or her deepest identity.

I remember weeping as I watched a crowning ceremony on television orchestrated by Oprah Winfrey. African-American women elders such as Dr. Maya Angelou, Coretta Scott King, Diahann Carroll, Toni Morrison, Nikki Giovanni, and Rosa Parks were honoured by "the young'uns", who recited Pearl Cleage's powerful poem, "We Speak your Names."

Two other celebrations stand out in my mind. One is an evening which my sister-friend Betsy and her family arranged for her 92 year old mother, Betty. After a wonderful meal in Betsy's home, a power point was shown of Betty's life, and a granddaughter presented her with an album of photos which were a biography from her birth to the present time. She was deeply touched.

John and I attended a wonderful 65th anniversary party for a couple in their late 80's, Pat and David. It was held on a lovely outdoor patio of a stately old hotel on a hot summer day. Four generations including their six children celebrated their lives with original songs, stories, and jokes, and of course a fabulous cake.

A Soulful Surprise
During John's final trip to California, one of the highlights was our visit to WDI, for which he had worked for seventeen years, including his six years at Tokyo Disney.

On the ride from Pasadena to Glendale, John repeated that he wished we had planned to call more of his Disney friends, as he would just love to find out about the projects they were doing now. He pushed his bright red walker into the familiar lobby at WDI. Senior Vice President Joe Lanzisero, whom he had called just the day before, greeted us warmly and escorted us down the hall toward the cafeteria. When we got there, Joe said, "Actually we're having lunch elsewhere", and we followed him to a large conference room. Seated around the table were twenty imagineers, colleagues throughout John's career, including some from Japan.

The walls were covered with photos of John on his many projects at Disneyland, Disney World in Florida and Tokyo Disney as well. There was also a table laden with a steaming Japanese buffet.

How they pulled this off within 24 hours from our call I can only attribute to Disney magic.

After a sumptuous meal, Joe asked each person there to say something about their current project and a few words about their time working with John. John was in awe, as each person acknowledged his virtues. Several said that he was "the quintessential gentleman", "a man of exquisite courtesy", "genuine integrity", "elegant and eloquent." Some said that their best work experience had been when John mentored or partnered with them. "Every now and then, if you're lucky," one young colleague said, "you get to stand on the shoulders of giants. John, you were mine. You were foundational in my career."

Several pointed out that beyond being creatively gifted, John "had such a way with people." He had taught them the importance of people as well as projects, and was a "bridge between cultures" in Japan. Some said they were still using the ACT with Tact Positivity Sandwich of The Virtues Project that John had taught them to use in performance appraisals.

At one point, many of us, including John, were on the precipitous verge of tears, when thankfully, a fellow shouted out, "Say, what kind of a roast is this anyway?" The laughter was a welcome release for everyone in the room.

John was amazed by these tributes. On the drive back to the hotel, he said, "I had no idea of the impact I had had on them." He added, "I'm aware of God's grace directing every day and every hour of these days. Every day has been so special. It's not that we'll miss it. We'll cherish it."

The Close-Up

John said, "Well, this has been a death-changing experience! I don't know how long I have but I'm about three months past my sell-by date!" Once the laughter subsided, he continued. "I have often spoken in this very room of a metaphor from the film industry, about the wide shot, the medium shot and the close-up." He explained that the wide shot is the big picture, the environment, what's happening in the world. The medium is relationships. The close-up is the most intimate view – illuminating the individual, the personal – where a facial expression reflects one's inner world.

He said that in the past, he had spoken about the state of the world – the wide shot. "This has been an extraordinary experience from a spiritual perspective, because it has helped me narrow my focus from human doing to human being. It has really focused my attention on the essential relationship, which is between the human soul and the Creator...Prayer is so much more meaningful to me now. I've had questions for God, and I often find myself breaking into tears. When you pray and when you listen, many magical things happen."

What I learned in companioning John was that his tears were not so much of sadness but of tenderness, awe and gratitude. "The encounter of the close-up with God has become central for me," he said. "It is completely redefined for the rest of my life. Religious scholars may underestimate how critical – and how near that relationship is." At times he wept softly, as did others in the room. "The words in the sacred texts have so much more meaning now. They aren't just suggestions. They're directions...and promises."

Radical Trust

Referring to the attraction he designed at Disneyland, and his childhood totem, John said, "I almost thought of calling this talk, 'Mr. Toad's Wild Ride.' It was a complete change in my script when I GOT it that I have no control over how long I have to live.

"Friends ask me if I'm afraid, but fear has never been a part of this for me. They ask if I have any hope. It's not about fear or hope. It's about trust. A scripture says that love and fear cannot abide in the same heart. It's an adventure. You have no idea what's next. And believe me, some of the adventures in the hospital would make an amazing movie – a horror film! And not a culinary movie by any means," he added. "For me," he continued, "trust is the critical virtue. He said, "The gifts are so much bigger than the challenges. I guess love precedes trust – the belief that God's not out to get me. There's this overriding theme in my life. The rest is ripples on the pond. The theme is God's plan for me. I watch God's bounty unfold every day. And death will be a reunion with the Beloved and so many marvellous souls I've known in this world." Afterwards, one woman said, "This has been the most transformational night of my life. I will never be the same." John beamed.

The Zen of Surrender

Shortly after we returned home, John decided to reprise his talk for our local community in his own living room. He called it, "The View from Spirit Lodge." When he first moved into this house, he had named it that, and designed a wrought iron entry gate with those words carved in it.

The place was packed, including every inch of floor space. Someone in the back said, "I can't see. Where's John?" "Just look for the two Q-Tips," said our friend Derek, referring to John's and my silver hair. John roared with laughter as did everyone else. We were recording his talk, and that huge laugh is the first thing you hear. (Go to www.gracefulendings.net to hear John's last lectures.)

After John spoke, there were questions. The first one was, "How do you accept the unacceptable?" John said, "I have a deeper understanding of the words, 'Nothing but that which profiteth them can befall My loved ones.' Acceptance was made easier by turning it over. I just turned it over. When you're trapped in one position by all the wires and tubes in hospital, you can either fight it, react to it in real time or surrender. It's a willful acceptance of difficulty. For me it feels like transcendence, being lifted above, going somewhere else. I was never a master of meditation. It just didn't stick. But it came in handy at every step. You just surrender to the Zen of the experience."

John began to go into detail about the tubes and nasty procedures in the hospital. I whispered "TMI, John." (too much information) He ended with an imitation of himself, "Enough said. 'You're putting WHAT WHERE?'" Everyone roared. He added, "I made up a little expression for when the nurses would come to give me a shot: 'Grab and stab', to make it easier on everyone. And believe me, after eight months on steroids, there's a lot more to grab!"

Creative Suffering
"Another lesson I received was about the nature of suffering. When I asked people at the Cancer Lodge 'How do you describe your cancer, they all said, "It's a gift." What an attitude of grace. That gives you pause. What am I meant to get from this? It wasn't in my script. Clearly it is God's will.

"Normal life may not challenge you much. The nature of suffering is a school for learning about your character in a way that grows your spiritual capacity. So, it is a gift, really." He went on to say, "It's a creative response to suffering as opposed to shame. Wisdom comes from education and suffering." John's last words on the recording that night were, "It's an exercise of trust. That's the bottom line."

Honor Their Gifts
Not everyone is a speaker in their spare time like John , but everyone is gifted in some way. A friend of mine who died recently at 93 had a lifelong passion for Esperanto. If I asked him to talk about it or teach me some, he lit up. We read The Lord's Prayer in Esperanto at his funeral. My mother-in-law, Patricia Popov, continues at 85 to crochet angels for virtues enthusiasts around the world. Indigenous people have given her the name, "The Angelmaker".

A friend of mine had a surprise for me on my last visit before she died. I originally met her at hospice when her husband was dying years before. Jean was a fashionista. She exulted in pastel ensembles, preened in suits of magenta and midnight blue. I could always tell when she was coming down the hall by the click of her perfectly matched high heels.

The day of my last visit to her, I found her in bed with the covers tucked up around her chin. She was emaciated and pale, but I noticed she was fully made up. Suddenly with a grin and a flourish, she flung the covers off. She was dressed in pink from head to toe, including pale pink stockings and matching low heels. She said, "Today, I'd like to take you to tea." I supported her as we slowly inched our way to the kitchen where tea had been laid out by her daughter.

After a while, Jean looked at me sadly and said, "I wish I'd been more like you." "How do you mean, Jean?" I asked. "I wish I'd been less vain, more virtuous." "Jean, to me, you are the epitome of virtue. You are the goddess of a virtue." She looked mystified. "Beauty!", I said. "In everything you do, and wear and surround yourself with in this lovely home, you celebrate the virtue of beauty." Her face lit up in a smile.

Shortly after that visit, she died. I was asked to speak at her funeral and as I looked out at the assembled mourners, I noticed attractive silver-haired women dressed to the nines throughout the congregation. Over refreshments, I discovered they were all members of Jean's fashion club.

"My friends, love is better than anger. Hope is better than fear. Optimism is better than despair. So let us be loving, hopeful and optimistic. And we'll change the world."
Excerpt from the last letter of Jack Layton, beloved Canadian politician who died of cancer at 61.

SUSTAINING VIRTUES:

Acceptance is embracing life on its own terms. We are open to what is rather than wishing for something different. We face the truth in all circumstances with honesty and courage. Acceptance helps us to bend without breaking in the winds of tests, to gather the lessons and step forward with new wisdom and awareness. We accept the things we cannot change. Acceptance brings us serenity.

Creativity is the power of imagination. We are open to inspiration, which ignites our originality. Discovering our own special talents is a gift to the world, whether making a meal, playing a sport, or creating a craft. Creativity connects us to beauty of sound, design, color, movement, ideas and words, and allows us to bring something new into the world. Creativity brings our gifts to fruition. It is the flowering of our souls.

HEALING STEPS:

1. Whatever they love or know, engage your loved one in doing it, talking about it, or teaching it. Connect with what is meaningful to them.

2. Consider how to create opportunities for the dying person to serve, even if it is just to pass on an idea by storying with them about it.

VI GETTING TO GOODBYE

"Endurance is not just the ability to endure a hard thing,
but to turn it into glory."
William Barclay, Scottish theologian

When one has received a terminal diagnosis, it often brings a titanic shift in priorities. There are decisions to be made and hopes to be honored.

How do we say goodbye to each other? What about the ongoing needs of the living? How should they be provided for? What happens to the family dynamics in this momentous process of letting go and saying goodbye? What can we expect as death approaches? Are there ways to know when it is about to happen?

Whatever else death is – frightening, comforting, inviting, horrifying – it is also fascinating. In light of the sheer finality of one's life in the physical world, death itself becomes a powerful presence.

Quantity or Quality

It basically involves whether or not we want to be kept alive for as long as possible no matter what, regardless of our level of suffering or the expense, which can be astronomical, in countries without universal health care coverage, such as the United States.

Some individuals wish to have exceptional measures taken until their last breath. To them, living as long as possible is the goal, regardless of having to endure invasive procedures. Others, as John did, prefer to be allowed to die with only palliative care – comfort and pain management the only measures taken. For John, issues of privacy, dignity, and a strong faith in the afterlife were the deciding factors. What matters here is using our right to choose while we can think clearly about such important issues.

One of our last acts of kindness to a dying person is respecting their right to choose how life will end in terms of how they want to be treated. When Jean, the fashionista, was dying, I gave her a small gift-wrapped box. Inside there was a smooth pink stone and a small white eagle heart feather. I told her, "When you feel you want to stay grounded on earth, you can hold this stone. When you feel you are ready to fly, you can hold the feather." This choice became a nightly ritual for her. In her last days, she chose flight.

Five Wishes

There is a simple document created by Jim Towey, called *The Five Wishes*, which beautifully and simply captures everything we need to decide before we die. It can be downloaded, signed, and filed with your will. *www.agingwithdignity.org/forms/5wishes.pdf*

For twelve years, Towey worked closely with Mother Theresa, including spending a year in a hospice she ran in Washington, D.C. *The Five Wishes* came from his desire to find a way to help families cope with serious illness. The response has been overwhelming. The document has been featured on CNN and NBC's Today Show. Newspapers have called *The Five Wishes* "the first living will with a heart and soul."

Wish 1: The Person I Want to Make Care Decisions for Me When I Can't

This section is an assignment of a health care agent (also called proxy, surrogate, representative or health care power of attorney.) This person makes medical decisions on your behalf if you are unable to speak for yourself.

Wish 2: The Kind of Medical Treatment I Want or Don't Want

This section is a living will—a definition of what life support treatment means to you, and when you would and would not want it.

Wish 3: How Comfortable I Want to Be

This section addresses matters of comfort care – what type of pain management you would like, personal grooming and bathing instructions, and whether you would like to know about options for hospice care, among others.

Wish 4: How I Want People to Treat Me

This section speaks to personal matters, such as whether you would like to be at home, and whether you would like someone to pray at your bedside.

Wish 5: What I Want My Loved Ones to Know

This section deals with matters of forgiveness, how you wish to be remembered and final wishes regarding funeral or memorial plans. My husband Dan has firm instructions about protecting me on my death bed from growing a handlebar mustache. I have waxed it off for so many years, I have no idea what it would look like if allowed to grow. I once encountered a woman at hospice who kept fingering the stubble on her upper lip. I said, "What's going on with your upper lip?" She whispered, in a horrified tone, "Mustache! They won't let me shave it." I said, "Let me see what I can do." I pushed her wheelchair back to her room, the two of us giggling wildly. I went to the nurse and told her the problem. She said, "Aren't you in charge of spiritual care?" I said, "That's what this IS!" She laughed and said, "Okay, she can use an electric razor, if you watch her." The danger was that if she cut through the skin, there

Forgiveness

The second virtue that presents a task for us when we are dying is forgiveness.

I companioned a man at hospice who had a long-standing feud with his brother. They had been estranged for more than forty years, and he felt quite hopeless about it. Although he thought about nothing else, he didn't feel he could actually contact his brother. I asked him what would be the best thing that could happen. "We would be together again. But I don't think he will forgive me." "You really care about your brother," I said, "What would give you the courage to let him know?" Within forty-eight hours, his brother was at his bedside, wrapping him in a long embrace. They both wept and shared that sacred moment of forgiveness.

When people find the courage to reconnect and heal old wounds with a simple act of forgiveness, it brings redemptive relief, a joyful spiritual freedom.

Gratitude

John's pain broke through in the last ten days of his life. He took this as a sign that the end was near. Once we managed to give him some relief with the right medications, his first thought was about what he had left to do before he died – who did he need to say goodbye to and who did he need to thank. John's unfinished business at this point was all about his pressing desire to express appreciation to the people that had impacted his life. As his "social secretary", I dialled the numbers, then left to give him privacy. From the next room, I could hear his huge belly laugh, and there were also tears of joy and sorrow as he shared with his closest friends and family members.

My friend Matt's eyes misted over as he told me about a time he was visiting his father in hospital in his last days, when suddenly his father said, "I'm so lucky." Matt was thinking "How do you figure that, Dad? You're dying of cancer!" but he chose to say: "How so, Dad?" His father went on: "I have you guys. I've had a great life, what more can you ask? What could be better?"

"What are you grateful for?" is a great companioning question. People get a sweet, wistful look on their faces, and always, in my experience, begin to talk about the things and the people they have loved.

The day before he died, John was comatose much of the time. I continued to talk him and ask him from time to time how he was doing. Several times, to my surprise, he rose up from the depths of coma and answered. One time, he responded, eyes still closed, "I was thinking how lucky we are, to be part of a wonderful global network that is always on call." Two hours later, he said those unforgettable words of gratitude that we had shared this journey together, and that it was perfect.

Last Prayer
There is a simple prayer to say for a dying person or to invite them to say with you if they are conscious. It can also be used if they are not conscious. The family and other caregivers can join in as well. It is based on a practice by Polynesian cultures from Hawaii to New Zealand, called Ho'oponopono, which means "to put right" or "make amends."

You can offer it by saying, "There is a simple prayer we can say together if you'd like. Repeat after me.
"I love you. I love you.
I forgive you. I forgive you.
Forgive me. Forgive me.
Thank you. Thank you.
Goodbye. Goodbye."

> *"An eye for an eye makes the whole world blind."*
> Mahatma Gandhi, Indian leader

SUSTAINING VIRTUES:

Love – The connection between one heart and another. Attraction, affection and caring for a person, a place, an idea, and for life itself.

Forgiveness – Overlooking mistakes. The willingness to move forward with a clean slate. Forgiving others frees us from resentment. Forgiving ourselves is an act of spiritual growth.

Gratitude is freely expressing appreciation to others. It is being thankful for the gifts of life.

HEALING STEPS:

1. Companion by asking open-ended questions, such as "Who has been important to you?" "What have you loved most in your life?" "What are you grateful for?" "Is there anyone you want to thank?"

2. Be mindful and alert to the dying person's need to communicate with people from his or her past or to make amends to family members or others. Facilitate communication if you can.

3. As they do their life review, avoid rationalizing their pain away. Be present to the meaning of what they are saying. That is enough. Simply hear them with respect.

4. Acknowledge them for the virtues you see – their honesty, their courage, their truthfulness.

24 FAMILY DYNAMICS

*"Lots of people are thrilled about the families they came from,
others couldn't get away fast enough."*
Paul Reiser, *Familyhood*

I'm going to be truthful. When someone is dying, it brings out
the worst in people, and the best. The dynamics that have always
existed – and every family has them – do not come to an end at the
end of life. They become more intense.

Dynamics involve the behaviour patterns and typical interactions
between people – the family drama, or the script, as John would
say. I am the eldest and had always been the family caregiver, John
was the clown and the pacifier, Dan was the head of the family from
the time he was born. First Nations people in Manitoba call him
"the lion watching over his pride."

I remember a case study that Hospice Victoria had given me when I
was applying for the job of Spiritual Care Coordinator. It described
a dying patient who was constantly cranky and complained about
everything the nurses did for her. On top of that she was refusing
to attend her daughter's wedding even though she could have
managed it in a wheelchair. "Well," I said during the interview, "this
woman has probably been in a snit all her life, and dying hasn't
changed that." To the amusement of the large panel of physicians,
department heads, and nurses, I added, "Basically, she needs a
'featherectomy.'" I couldn't believe that had come out of my mouth.
What must that have said about my notions of spiritual care? After
the laughter died down, they must have decided that I fit the bill,
because I was offered the job the next day.

Soon after, I learned that this woman was not just a fictional case.
Most of the spiritual care I offered her consisted of joking with her
about her demands, and getting her to laugh. I companioned her
about the heart of the matter in her concerns about the wedding,
and found out that she was embarrassed about her extraneous tubes

condition, or if he preferred to be spared. He instantly replied that he wanted to know every detail. I'm glad to say that through our many talks during the days before John died, and afterwards, a new closeness grew between us, which has remained and deepened. There is a new acceptance of our differences, and joy in sharing the humor unique to our family.

Make Sure the Medical Proxy is Appointed

Every terminally ill person needs to be asked who they feel most comfortable being their medical representative if the time comes when they lose consciousness or are no longer capable of making their wishes known. This may have nothing to do with family rank. One woman revealed to me privately that she preferred her younger daughter to be in that role as her older daughter was so opinionated. She was afraid that she would follow her own ideas rather than listen to her mother.

Follow the Lead of the Primary Caregiver

Family members need to respect the decisions made by the patient and the primary caregiver rather than creating needless conflict by arguing over every issue. It's one thing to gently offer a perspective or idea, leaving the decision to the two of them, and another to argue and badger. At a time like this, being unified is more important than being right.

Be a Peacemaker

Avoid the temptation to judge and talk about each other behind backs. If you have a problem, address it directly with the person involved – gently and tactfully. Having a loved one who is critically ill is stressful enough. Do not make matters worse by bringing your personal animosity toward another family member into the situation. Be inclusive. If the individual is willing to see people, let them come. Give each family member time alone with the dying person if possible. This allows for real heart to heart communication rather than the more superficial chat or a "death watch" atmosphere of a group surrounding the individual.

Go with the Flow

As the dying process progresses, let it be what it is. Summon your detachment. When a family member is dying, it is not the time to add to the drama with your opinions when they differ from that of the patient and the primary caregiver. It is not a time for grandstanding. Remember that the individual is going to die one way or another. Accepting the decisions that are made is really the most helpful stance to take, whether or not you agree with them. Your job is to be a peace-maker and a unifier, making the remaining days of your family member as graceful as possible.

"Blessed are the peacemakers
for they shall be called the children of God."
Mathew 5:9

SUSTAINING VIRTUES:

Humility is being open to every lesson life brings, trusting that our mistakes are often our best teachers. We realize that our perspective and our needs are no more important than those of others.

Respect is an attitude of honoring oneself and others through our words and actions. We treat every person with dignity and courtesy.

Unity is inclusiveness. It is finding common ground in our diversity. We seek peace in all circumstances.

HEALING STEPS:

1. Call on your humility and respect for the dying person and the primary caregiver to accept the things you wish were different. Having strong feelings doesn't mean it is helpful to express them.

2. Avoid going on automatic and jumping into the typical role you play in the family. Breathe. Observe. Be deeply considerate of each person involved.

3. If your family culture is open to it, hold a Virtues Sharing Circle. Each person shares briefly, without any cross talk, just receptive silence on the part of the others, in response to questions such as: What saddens me? and What am I most grateful for? Or "A thorn and a rose". Then the person on either side gives the one who has just shared a virtues acknowledgment. "I see your commitment to Dad. You have always been there for him." This is a deeply unifying activity.

4. Depending on your beliefs, sing and pray together with or around the dying person.

25 GLIMPSES OF ETERNITY

"Another world is not only possible, she is on her way.
On a quiet day, I can hear her breathing."
Arundhati Roy, Indian novelist

As I have said, I find that people who are near death often have amazing wisdom and spiritual lucidity. As their executive powers wane, their spiritual perceptiveness seems to deepen. Asking them questions can often bring forth surprisingly discerning and even visionary answers.

A question I like to ask is, "Will you give me some personal advice? What do you think is most important in my life right now?" When I asked this of Jean, the fashionista, she didn't skip a beat, saying, "You need to finish your next book." As far as I knew, she didn't even know I was writing a book at the time and certainly not the fact that I had stalled out. I immediately got back to work on A Pace of Grace.

Between Worlds
It is also very common for dying individuals to experience visitations or intimations from souls in the next world. John was no exception. He had premonitions and some dramatic experiences just prior to his death as, in his words, he "straddled both worlds".

Three days before he died, he said at breakfast, "Lin, we'd better catch that hummingbird." "What hummingbird?" I asked. "The one that just flew by." "Hmm, how do you know it went by?" I asked. He said, "I heard the wings." Wings, I thought, they're coming for him.

He went on to say, "The pull of this world and the pull of the next world are exactly equal now." His eyes were shining in anticipation. "You're halfway there, John," I said. He added, "I'm just longing for a hand up." He went in the living room to nap in his recliner and came back at lunchtime with an odd expression on his face. "Something very bizarre and mystical just happened. I hope you won`t think

I`m crazy." "I'd think you're crazy?" "Oh, right," he grinned, remembering my own propensity to mysticism. "Dad came and put his hand on my shoulder and said, 'I will help you come home.'" We sat in silence, taking in the mystery of the moment. Then I said, "There's the hand you asked for." We both cried.

A few days before, when he was resting in the living room at night, reading prayers, he told me later, "The whole room was full of souls, so radiant and beautiful, just swirling around me. It was very positive, very joyful."

Worlds Touch

Even if I did not have a lifelong belief in life after death, I have been blessed to witness moments with the dying that I don't believe can be explained otherwise.

A call came into hospice from a woman whose husband was on the waiting list for admission. He had suddenly died at home the night before. The social worker and I drove out to see her and found her very quiet, unemotional, but with a lot of practical questions. I sat across from them as the social worker talked to her about funeral arrangements. Suddenly the scent of flowers filled the room, and I looked around, but there were no flowers. Beside her a tall figure appeared, outlined in light. I could see his high forehead and full face. He looked to be in his early 40's. He was raising his arms up with an ecstatic smile, saying to her, "I'm so happy!" I sat in wonder, watching to see if they could see him as well, but they simply carried on. I wrote her telephone number in my daybook.

Before we left, I asked, "Do you have a picture of your husband?" She left briefly to retrieve it. To my amazement, there was the man I had seen but about thirty years older in his photo. Once we were settled in the car, the social worker said to me, "Linda, you're shaking. What is it? Did you have one of your woo-woo experiences?" I told him what had occurred. He had seen nothing. He smiled and shook his head. Six months later, I sensed it was time to call the widow. She remembered our visit. I asked her how she was doing. "Well, I just keep wondering if he's happy," she said. I told her about the vision I had seen, and could feel her smile over the phone.

There is a good deal of research on near death experiences, including that of early pioneer in the field, Raymond Moody, which point to the existence of a spiritual realm. The world's sacred texts testify to our ongoing spiritual existence. My own experiences with the dying confirm my faith in that reality.

I have often had the experience, while I was away or at home, of feeling the sudden, profound presence of someone at the moment of their death. One morning I was out on my deck praying when a man I had been companioning for weeks appeared beside me, like a waking dream figure. He said, "Linda, I'm going! It's so beautiful! Pray me over." This from a man who claimed to have no faith in life after death. Stunned, I began to pray for him. I glanced at my watch and noted that it was 7:24 AM. That afternoon, his son rang me and said, "Linda, we wanted you to know that Dad passed away this morning." "What time?" I asked, "Just before 7:30," he said.

A Perfect Day
The day before John's final seizure, he had a perfect day. Friends of mine called, saying they wanted to come to the island and take me out for coffee. They were hours away but were coming to give me support. "Who's that?" John called out. "Two of my favourite friends." "Oh, Kara and Cheryll?" he said. I was astonished that out of all my friends, he would know who was on the phone. There was that clairvoyance I had witnessed in other dying people, including my father. "Are they bringing the cello?" he asked. "Why?" they wanted to know. "John wants you to bring it." "Then we will." They turned around, and drove back to pick it up.

Dan and I took John out for a picnic lunch, getting some of his favourite burgers and greasy fries to go. When we got to the park, he was too fatigued to get out of the car, so we said, "Okay, John, let's go to our house." I was planning his favourite dinner for that night and needed to make it in my own kitchen.

He was very unstable, even on his walker, but we helped him into the house and he sat quietly taking in the view from the home we three had shared years before. "The beauty of this view is almost unbearable," he said, gazing out at the ocean below, sailboats gliding by, and snow-clad Mount Baker glistening in the sun. I noticed that for several days, his sense of beauty had become deeper, more intense.

Later, I took him into the bedroom for a rest while I prepared dinner. He was very restless. He kept calling out, "Lin, what are we doing? Where are we going?" So, I brought him out to sit with me while I made southern fried chicken, potato salad and fresh green beans with mushrooms. Dan's mother Pat had mailed us one of John's favourite desserts, which we couldn't get in Canada – two chocolate Hostess Cupcakes wrapped in cellophane. Miraculously, Canada Post delivered them in time and intact. John savoured every morsel.

Dan did the dishes, and then we left to return to John's where our friends were going to meet us after dinner. He was completely unable to steer his walker back to the car, and I thought, "He's really changing."

Kara, who is an accomplished and gifted cellist, often a soloist for the Yakima, Washington symphony, played for John that night. He and I both wept. What a perfect send-off. Cheryll had brought her camera, and when she was taking John's last photo, I said, "Smile, John," and his face lit up in a radiant smile. He then took a photo of the three of us, which was tilted. We cherish it, of course. When they left, he said, "It doesn't get any better than this." Two days later he was gone.

"Death, be not proud, though some have called thee
Mighty and dreadful, for thou art not so...
One short sleep past, we wake eternally,
And death shall be no more; Death, thou shalt die."
Excerpted from *Death Be Not Proud* by poet John Donne

SUSTAINING VIRTUES:

Wonder – Being open to the beauty and mysteries of life and of death. Our soul's appreciation for what is precious and inspiring.

Faith is a relationship of trust. It is belief in the reality of Grace.

HEALING STEPS:

1. Companion people in their last hours as gently and unobtrusively as you can. Just be a listening, witnessing presence. They may be experiencing mysteries beyond your understanding.

2. Trust the images or messages that may come to you softly through the veil.

26 SIGNS OF THE END

"This is love: to fly toward a secret sky,
to cause a hundred veils to fall each moment.
First to let go of life. Finally, to take a step without feet."
Jalal'u'din Rumi, Sufi mystic poet

John's new script was that of a dying man who was not merely embracing the unknown, but awaiting it with open arms. Most of the people I have cared for at hospice met death with a sense of peace. Yet, I had never before witnessed such joy. The palliative care nurses told me and John the same thing.

Waiting with Grace
During our last visit to the local palliative care physician, aptly named Dr. Crossland, he said, "I have never seen anyone meet death with such peace...Why?" John paused thoughtfully. "Well, I've always loved change – enjoyed the new. In our Faith, prayer is conversation with the Beloved, and death is reunion with the Beloved. So for me, there's no fear. There's never been any fear. To be honest, I can hardly contain my excitement about what's next." The silence in the room deepened as John's twin Tommy and I wept silently. John just beamed.

John had outlived all the predictions of the oncologists who said that at his age, with this aggressive tumor, he had more or less three months to live. As the fifteen months stretched out, every medical person hinted at his imminent demise. Their surprise each time they saw him was palpable. Several months before he died, our primary care doctor took me aside and said, "Linda, John is so, so on borrowed time."

Living in the Moment
How do you wait in a life-affirming way, when you know the end is near? One day, during our sacred time, John said, "I'm getting exhausted from treading water and holding my breath about what's coming, as if I am going to keel over any moment. You can't just

tread water forever." He added, with a grin, "All that bated breath waiting to be released."

As his closest companion, I was utterly spent from my own hyper-vigilance – listening for him in the night, checking on his breathing. I hadn't had one night of deep, restful sleep in ages. I was constantly on the alert, preparing myself for the end. "What do you need John?" I asked. "I need to move forward!" he said. "It isn't easy to live with this uncertainty. We need to commit to the NOW!" I said, "Okay, John, let's do it." We both took a deep breath of patience and relaxed.

One morning, John said, "Rhythm is the word that comes to me today – getting back into the groove, not compulsively, but creatively." The words of Albert Einstein came to mind: "Life is like riding a bicycle. To keep your balance, you have to keep moving." It was after the decision to live in the moment that John was miraculously able to finalize the new Virtues Project website design.

One to Three Months Before Death
There are recognizable changes toward the end of life. They vary with each person, yet there are natural patterns that occur, from sleep patterns to appetite and mood shifts. They may ask for a special favorite food, as John often did, then say it doesn't taste right.

As they begin to accept their mortality and realize that death is approaching, they may withdraw, becoming more quiet and contemplative. They are often preoccupied with sorting through memories and regrets. They are starting the process of detaching from the world and their relationships. They are often very focused on final tasks such as telling a loved one what to do with their belongings or their car, concrete things that are small gifts of thoughtfulness. They give things away.

My friend Jackie's husband Doug, knowing her love for travel, talked to her often in his last weeks about using their Frequent Flier miles to go somewhere after his death. In his final hours, he kept repeating "miles, miles."

John often spent time resting in his last days, seemingly lost in thought. He was reflecting deeply on the things he appreciated about me and Dan, and others close to him. He talked about our brother Tommy's virtues, his sweetness. On their birthday, which was his last, he painstakingly wrote out a long letter telling Tommy everything he loved about him. Meanwhile, Tommy had done the same for John.

Last Week to Two Weeks
In the last week or two, attitudes about visitors may change. The dying person may not want to see people that before they had welcomed to their bedside, even family members. The primary caregiver has to call on tact and wisdom to manage the flow of visitors at a time when the needs of others and the needs of the dying person may differ.

The dying person may experience reduced appetite and weight loss as the body begins to slow down. The body doesn't need the energy from food that it once did. Before you whip out their favourite dessert in an effort to tempt their appetite, realize that this is part of the letting go process. The body does a wonderful thing during this time as altered body chemistry produces a mild sense of euphoria. When someone is neither hungry nor thirsty, they are not suffering in any way by not eating. It is a natural part of getting ready for death.

John was the exception to the rule. He ate heartily until his very last day. This may have been the effect of being on a steroid, which stimulates appetite. And rather than weight loss that many cancer patients experience, he was heavier than he had ever been in his life.

Somnolence, or sleeping for long periods day and night, is common during the last weeks. Disorientation and altered perceptions can be expected. It is best to go along with these imaginings in the sense that you are offering help or comfort based on what the person is perceiving. Help them to cope as best you can. Mirroring their gestures is a gentle way to companion them. My sister-in-law would make circles with her finger, so I did the same, and she managed a weak smile.

There is often a surge of energy just before death. Our next door neighbour and long-time friend, George, spent all day every day with his wife Eunice in hospital before she died. The day before she passed, they experienced what he considers a small miracle. She had been lying there, silent for days, and that day her eyes were glued to the ceiling. Then she shut them and never opened them again. Suddenly her voice filled the room. George was startled by the sheer volume of her voice, because she hadn`t spoken for days and normally she was very soft-spoken. ``Kiss me!" she said. He moved from the foot of her bed to take her in his arms, and recited lines from the 23rd Psalm to her, "Thou shalt fear no evil". He told her, "There is nothing to fear. You will wait for me in heaven until I come to you." And then he kissed her. She died later that night.

It is NOT helpful to talk people out of their perceptions when they don't fit normal reality. I learned this at hospice when nurses would go in and try to calm someone who was reacting loudly to delusions. They would ask me to go and "do that thing you do or we'll have to give her a shot." One woman was shouting obscenities about this "f-in place", pacing her room like a mad woman. I went into her room, raised my voice to match her tone, and yelled, "What's going on in here? What about this f-in place?" The woman stopped suddenly with an expression of relief as if to say, "Finally, someone who speaks my language." "What kind of a f-in place won't feed the dogs?" "What? They won't feed the dogs?" I said. I saw that she was looking around the room at imaginary animals. The nurse had said, "This is a clean place. We don't have any dogs," and threatened her with a shot if she didn't "calm down." I gave her a virtues acknowledgment: "You care about the dogs." She smiled. I asked her, "What do you think we can do about this?" "Feed them!" she said victoriously. She began to make hand motions, which I imitated. She then collapsed into my arms, murmuring, "Thank you." Soon after she was back in bed completely peaceful again.

In the last week or so, there is a restlessness that sets in. During the last couple of nights before he died, John was obsessing about his cat, wandering the house looking for her. It was strange that she was still out, because normally she didn't leave his side. "We have to get her in. She's lost," he'd say. I promised him I would go out and find her. He calmed enough to get into bed, but kept popping up again until Misha came to snuggle beside him.

During their last days, many dying persons experience the presence of someone who has died, often a relative or close friend. Some believe this is a veil being lifted between this life and the next, as John did when he felt our father's hand on his shoulder. In their agitation, they make gestures, such as picking at the covers or their clothes. They talk about having to go somewhere. John said, "Where are we going? We have to go." I have heard others talk about "going around the corner. I just have to go around the corner." It is best to listen respectfully and repeat to them, "Time to go?" They may feel confused if you try to take it further by asking "Where are you going?" Just let it be.

One woman told her husband on their last outing a few days before she died, "I don't have to pack my bags, you know." Then she repeated it as she lay in bed, going in and out of consciousness. "I meant it you know. I don't have to pack." Ways to respond are not to interrogate the individual but to repeat it as if you understand. "Oh, you don't have to pack a thing." Meeting them in this way helps them to feel understood.

Final Hours
There are signs that the body is beginning to shut down. There is a new level of weakness and instability. Consciousness begins to change as well, with confusion and speaking about things others

cannot understand. Many dying people are completely somnolent, sleeping almost around the clock in their last hours.

On his last night at home, John was very restless. I found myself checking on him throughout the night. At 5 AM, I found him terribly agitated, trying to get out of bed, saying, "I have to go. I have to go." I held his walker steady and did my best to bring him to a standing position. Somehow, he turned sideways, stretched out his arms and did a swan dive backwards, hitting the floor hard. It was his last seizure. I called 911 and the first responders came, sirens blaring. I handed them his "Do Not Resuscitate" form we kept on the fridge. I followed the ambulance to the Emergency Room, where he was given a hefty dose of morphine, as he had a massive headache when he woke from the seizure.

I sat outside the ER, sobbing quietly, dried my eyes and went in to see him. "Lin, you put a capital G in Grace," he said. Shortly afterward he was transferred to the palliative care suite.

Physical Changes
As the body gradually stops maintaining itself, the body temperature lowers, and extremities become cold. Blood pressure lowers. The pulse becomes irregular and may speed up or slow down. Skin color changes as circulation slows. This is often more noticeable in the lips and nail beds, which become pale and take on a bluish tinge. Breathing changes, often becoming more rapid and labored. Congestion can occur causing a rattling sound and cough. Speaking decreases and eventually stops altogether. It is common for "Cheyne-Stokes" breathing to occur – rapid breaths followed by periods of no breathing. Then the rapid breaths begin again until, at last, they stop.

Sharon, the wonderful palliative care nurse who had been visiting us for months, called me on my cell phone, having learned that John was admitted to hospital. She said something that literally helped me through John's last night. "Linda, it could get ugly." And it did.

The room was anything but fragrant. There was blood coming from John's mouth, and the sound of his rattling breath. I tried to sleep in the bed provided for relatives, but something else kept me awake as well. I heard music. Although it was quite a beautiful, gentle and plaintive chorus of voices, I went out into the hall to find out who was playing music at that late hour. The music wasn't coming from the hallway. It was inside the room. I knew there was nothing electronic on. I put earplugs in to stop listening to the music and to John's laboured breathing. The music became louder. It felt as though angels were giving him a welcome concert.

It is widely believed that the last sense to go is hearing. So, in those last hours, it is important to speak as if your loved one hears every word. Saying goodbye can be as simple as "I love you".

> *"My entire being gives itself over*
> *Ecstatically to His embrace*
> *Into the very heart*
> *Of beatitude."*
> Julia Esquivel, Mayan Indian author

SUSTAINING VIRTUES:

Awe is deep respect and reverence for the Source of life. It is humility and wonder before the power of God. Contemplating life's beauty and mystery leads us to communion. Reflecting on our place in the universe, we seem small and insignificant, yet it is awe-inspiring to realize that no one else on earth is just like us. When we practice awe, we are alert to the signs and wonders placed in our path. We open ourselves to Grace.

Serenity is tranquility of spirit. It is an abiding sense of trust and faith that all is well. In the midst of trials, we are accepting and resilient. We go with the flow. Serenity soothes our souls.

HEALING STEPS:

1. As best you can, surrender to what is happening in the present moment. If your loved one is able, plan something enjoyable for the day. Companion the dying person with detachment and compassion as they do their final life review or say their goodbyes. Make them as comfortable as possible. If they are sleeping and quiet, just be there. Concentrate on them with your love.

2. Meet the dying person in their reality. Gently comfort them based on what they are seeing, imagining or hearing.

3. Accept the physical and mental changes of the dying without alarm or an attempt to keep them alive. It is not kind to prolong their death. This is the natural way of making the transition.

27 LAST BREATH

"If I had to choose between breathing and loving you
I would use my last breath
to tell you I love you."
DeAnna Anderson, poet

At hospice I often felt like a mid-wife to the dying. A nursing
colleague said to me, "You know, I've noticed that the energy in the
room when someone dies is the same as when a child is born." There
is a sacred kind of excitement about an approaching death. Being
present at that precious split second of transition is a privilege. Some
family members go for days without sleep not wanting to miss it.

My husband Dan had spent the morning before with John after
he was admitted to hospital. One of John's first questions after
he regained consciousness from the seizure was, "What's for
breakfast?" He ate heartily of toast and oatmeal. Perhaps because
this is so unusual in the last hours of life, the doctor told Dan that
he could last a long time, even weeks. The nurse, overhearing them,
took me aside later that day and said, "I don't think he has long at
all, Linda. I don't think he's going to make it." I immediately went
to get my overnight bag. Dan stayed until early evening and then
went back to John's house.

As the day wore on, John was no longer interested in food. I tried to
feed him some yoghurt but he wasn't interested. His headache was
severe and he was given as much morphine as he needed. He sank
deeper and deeper into a comatose state.

John was a left-handed man. After the intense seizure that led
to this hospitalization, his left side was completely paralyzed. I
noticed he kept reaching up with his right, perhaps seeking that
"hand up" he longed for.

His one fear had been that if he went into a coma, he would feel
claustrophobic, "but then I might not know I was in a coma so it

would be okay." In actuality as he drifted deeper into a comatose state, he seemed very peaceful. I alternated between a peaceful and often prayerful silence and talking and singing to him, saying his favourite prayers aloud. One was "Oh God, my God, my beloved, my heart's desire." I sang songs from our childhood, some from our Sunday School, and some Broadway tunes we loved.

There is a small courtyard with a fountain outside the palliative care suite. It was a balmy July morning and I went out to pray and do a Virtues Pick. I had been praying all night for a merciful end for John. I reached into the silk Kimono bag holding my Virtues Cards and pulled one out. It was Mercy. The quote on the card is from Shakespeare: "The quality of mercy is not strain'd; it droppeth as the gentle rain from heaven upon the place beneath…." I wept with gratitude.

Last Words
Once John seemed to completely lose consciousness, I asked that a sign be put up to prevent visitors. I didn't think John would like them to see him like this. But at one point, I heard John's voice in my head, saying, "Call Bryn and Carol," two very close friends of ours. I left a message on their answering machine, and soon, there they were. They both sing beautifully and we stood around John's bed and sang prayers for him. He no longer had any expression on his face, and was taking very regular, deep breaths, then he would pause. The three of us went out into the little courtyard for some fresh air, and sat on a bench talking for a couple of minutes, just a few feet from John's bed. We went back in and started another prayer, standing at the foot of his bed. Suddenly, Carol said, "He isn't breathing." "Wait for it," I said. But another breath never came. He had slipped away. I felt jubilant for him, raised my arms and said, "He did it!" The nurses came in and exulted with me. I rang Dan on my cell phone, and told him, "John just passed." He wept, saying, "The song that just played is, 'Take my hand, precious Lord.'"

What a mystery it is to witness a person breathing one moment and not breathing the next – just a whisper of difference.

John spoke his last words when our friends were visiting the night before he died. His eyes were closed and his voice was garbled but he distinctly said, "Class act." "What's a class act, John?" "You guys," he said and gave a lop-sided smile. John's life, and his death, could well be described in those very words.

"Oh my brother! Take thou the step of the spirit, so that, swift as the twinkling of an eye thou mayest flash through the wilds of remoteness and bereavement, attain the paradise of everlasting reunion, and in one breath commune with the heavenly Spirits."
Baha'u'llah, Prophet-Founder of The Baha'i Faith

SUSTAINING VIRTUES:

Faith is a relationship of trust. It is believing in the reality of Grace. Even in the most trying times, we are open to miracles.

Grace is our connection to the Divine, a sense that we are loved and provided for in all circumstances. It is opening ourselves to bounty. As we connect deeply with grace, we become the presence of grace to others.

HEALING STEPS:

1. Be the presence of grace to a dying person. Have a serene, peaceful spirit.

2. Trust. Have faith that all is well.

3. Don't leave anyone out who needs to be there. Connect with the people who want to know about your loved one's passing. It will mean the world to them.

VII LIFE AFTER DEATH

"Change is the egg of the phoenix."
Christina Baldwin, author

What kind of life can we expect after a death? What will happen to us in this part of the journey? How do we navigate the loss of one we have loved deeply? How can we handle the onslaught of grief while taking care of all the details that need to be handled?

Life will never be the same, yet it will go on. It will be different. We must give ourselves permission to live through this time of sorrow with compassion and even hope.

28 CEREMONY AND CELEBRATION

"Death is not extinguishing the light; it is putting out the lamp because the dawn has come."
Rabindranath Tagore, Hindu leader & author

The first thing we do after a loved one dies, is come together. We gather to honor their passing and to celebrate their life.

Immediately after John died, Dan and I had to quickly turn our attention to hosting family who were flying in from all over the world. Tommy and his wife arrived the next day, having taken the red eye from Puerto Rico. They flew in their daughters, my nieces Nava from Israel and Zhena from Stockholm. Dan and I moved out of John's home and back into ours ten minutes down the road, then prepared for all the relatives to move in to John's house. I needed my sons beside me, and they came – Craig from San Francisco and Chris from Australia. For most people, this time of finalizing plans for the funeral and often a memorial Celebration of Life some time later consumes all their energy. It can be a merciful deferral of grief.

Planning the Funeral
The ways we celebrate the life of one who has died are very personal. There can be a simple gathering around an urn containing the departed one's ashes or a burial attended only by the family. There can be an elaborate funeral to which many people are invited. It is also very tied in to whether or not the family is religious, since one's faith usually has prescribed rituals to be followed, and is often presided over by clergy.

Many people are used to leaving ceremonies in the hands of their rabbi, minister, or priest. They may not realize that a funeral can be as creatively and personally planned as a wedding. It does not have to be led by a member of the clergy.

The elements of the plan generally include the following:
1.   If the individual has requested certain things be done, those

of course need to be integrated into the ceremony.

2. The obituary needs to be written and sent to the local newspaper along with a photo of the deceased if the family so desires.

3. Order flowers for the burial or funeral.

4. Choose readings from scriptures, prayers, poetry, or passages that are meaningful to the deceased person.

5. Plan the music. Here in Canada and in other countries, we often bring in a piper to play the bagpipes as people enter the hall, church, or cemetery and as they leave.

6. Arrange for words of welcome to those assembled and words shared by individuals close to the departed.

7. Work with the Funeral Director about how the ceremony will proceed in the funeral home or at the burial site.

Be Creative

The burial laws of the Baha'i Faith are similar to those of Judaism and Islam, in that it should take place as soon after death as possible, preferably within 24 hours. Our burial ceremony for John was very simple. Close family and a few very close friends gathered with our Baha'i community in a circle around John's coffin in the cemetery. Tommy welcomed everyone, and we had a few prayers, and a passage from scripture sung by our friend Carol, who had witnessed John's last breath. People were invited back to John's home for refreshments, including John's favorite bakery cake, a rich chocolate ganache. We included in the obituary in our local paper an open invitation to a Celebration of Life several days later in a local hotel. Others prefer to have a formal funeral in a house of worship or funeral home followed by the burial, and perhaps a memorial gathering a year or more later.

When a man died rather suddenly in his forties, his friends got together, dressed him in a flannel shirt and overalls, transported him in a pick-up truck to a hall, where they had a keg of beer, and a display of some of his favorite things, wooden sculptures he had carved, and photos of him on hikes and climbing mountains. They served his favorite foods. Friends spoke of what they loved and admired about him.

When the father of one of my relatives died, they honored him in a way that was very personal. He was a loner, who drank beer and loved to fish on a nearby river. His four children and I drove up to the river and stood in a circle. One of them held his cremated remains. They asked me to say some words about him, and then each of them took a sip of his favourite beer. Then they poured his ashes and the rest of the beer into the river.

When 92 year old David died, most of his six children were off at a wedding of one of his grandsons several hundred miles away. After calling the Funeral Director to pick up David's body at the hospital, his wife Pat called me. She was quite conflicted about whether to go to the wedding as planned, or not. I companioned her. "What worries you about going to the wedding?" I asked. She didn't want to abandon her husband of 67 years. I told her, "His spirit is free now, and he can be with you wherever you are. What do YOU need? Do you want to have some time alone at home or do you want to be with your family?" She decided to go and two of her sons came to pick her up. When she arrived she said, "Now, no wailing and sympathizing. This is Josh's (the groom's) day. Let's just celebrate." Their children were overjoyed to have her there with them. Several days later, four generations of family gathered for a simple graveside ceremony for David. After a few readings, prayers and the Tennyson poem, "Crossing the Bar", David's son played Danny Boy on the guitar and we all sang. He had often accompanied his father, who played that beloved tune on the harmonica. I was not alone in wiping away tears. Each of us placed a rose on his coffin and the children remained to see his burial through as the rest of us left. Ten days later, they held a tea,

29 APPRECIATE THE ORDINARY

"Normal day, let me be aware of the treasure you are."
Mary Jean Iron, author

The intensity of waiting for death can be overwhelming. Then, when death comes, especially after a long illness, there is a gamut of emotions. One that surprised me was relief. As the primary caregiver, I was suddenly free of the constancy of meeting John's end of life needs, and the myriad responsibilities that crowded our days.

The Ebbing of Intensity

As I went about doing the many tasks to prepare for John's burial and celebration, calling family and friends, doing the banking, choosing the casket, I suddenly recognized a fresh sense of normalcy. I could write my task list and check things off without interruption. I would stand in a line at the bank and it would dawn on me, I didn't have to rush back to give John his meds. I was no longer anxious about his wellbeing.

The hyper-vigilance which had become a way of life for me magically disappeared. I breathed in the simplicity of the new normal, albeit a very busy day. The flurry of activity was soothing and mercifully numbing. I was still high with elation that John had escaped the narrow confines of his deteriorating body, his deepening pain and discomfort. I sensed his triumphant, joyous spirit soaring. I was happy for him.

It was a huge shift to be able to waken whenever I chose, to have a leisurely cup of coffee in blissful silence, to be off duty. Sitting with Dan having quiet conversation that wasn't focused on tragedy or problem solving was a fresh gift.

Guilt Free

When we begin to enjoy life again in these small ways, it is not unusual for guilt to arise. How can I lose this person I love and feel the least bit glad? Where is the grief I should be feeling? Wait for it. It will come.

So, give yourself full permission to feel whatever you feel. Enjoy the moments of quiet relief, which come with the return to life without the stress of terminal illness. Who would miss that?!

Natural Wonder
In the face of death, life seems more precious. A heightened sense of vitality and gratitude for just being alive is a natural reaction to loss. Life and death come to each of us, and when we lose someone close, that reality looms before us, perhaps for the first time.

Breathe in the pleasure of just being alive. No worries. You are not being unfaithful or disloyal to the one who has died. I believe that the respite simple pleasures bring is a gift both to the ones left behind and the person who is now in the spiritual realm. Perhaps it is a comfort to them to see joy in the ones they love.

"Tis a gift to be simple, tis a gift to be free."
Shaker elder Joseph Brackett

SUSTAINING VIRTUES:

Contentment is an awareness of sufficiency, a sense that we have enough and we are enough. It is appreciating the simple gifts of life – friendship, books, a good laugh, a moment of beauty, a cool drink on a hot day. It is a place to stand and view the future with a peaceful heart and gratitude for all that is and all that is to come.

Simplicity – Content with the basic gifts of life, we let go of excess, clutter and complexity. We savour the moment.

HEALING STEPS:

1. Allow yourself the small pleasures of returning to life without terminal illness at the center.

2. Detach from any guilt that arises. Just be thankful.

30 AFTERMATH

"You can't get over it. You can only get through it."
Dan Popov, Co-Founder of The Virtues Project

When the busy period after a death subsides, grief slips in and
fills in all the cracks and gaping holes in one's sense of normalcy.
One can experience feelings of unreality, disorientation and deep
sorrow. I always write notes of condolence around the six week
mark, because in my experience, that is when sadness hits most of
us who have lost someone we love.

First Wave
Ironically, just as the wave of grief smashes over us, this seems to
be the time when people expect us to get over it and get on with
life – get back to work, get past it, get back to normal. Yet the sense
of loss can be all-consuming. Each of us has to find our own way to
navigate this part of the journey.

For me, the grief of bereavement was a shape-shifter, unpredictable
in its form and frequency. It utterly disrupted my life. Although I
continued to function, to work on John's affairs, to fulfill his last
wish for Dan and me to complete the new website for The Virtues
Project, deep sorrow tainted everything. About eight weeks after
John's death, I wrote in my journal:

> *Today, I feel drained, literally had the runs. I am awash in tears.*
> *If you have been the caregiver, especially for an extended period*
> *of years, people secretly believe you are greatly relieved when the*
> *child or adult dies. But instead you find yourself bereft of your*
> *center of gravity, out of a job, having lost an intense sense of*
> *purpose, of being needed.*

Loss of Reality
When someone who has been a significant love in our lives suddenly
vanishes – and it always seems sudden, even when they have been ill
for a long time – it feels completely surreal. "What?!" our inner voice

screams. "How can he be gone?" Emotional thinking has nothing to do with what we know intellectually to be true. For me, there was a deeply disorienting sense that John's death wasn't real, therefore God and life after death weren't real. Lifelong beliefs held scant comfort and seemed a distant whisper in the wind, while storm clouds of anger and loss rumbled and surged within me.

Flat Lining

I journaled, "The death of feeling goes on and on." To me it felt like the heaviest boredom. Nothing satisfied or penetrated my deadened emotions. This was not the time to intrude with hope, to tell me that "this too shall pass". I needed people to meet me there, to honor my reality. As I have already said, it is a common mistake for people to try talking a grieving person out of their pain, to promise that it will be over one day. This only isolates us more and adds a layer of needless guilt to compound our grief. Only in being present to our experience with compassion and love can it heal. Saying, "Of course you're sad." "You must miss her terribly," validates our experience. We feel less alone.

I was grateful for the virtues of patience and understanding during the worst days of my bereavement, in others and in myself. I held my broken heart gently, knowing I could not rush the process. I had no choice about going through it. I could only choose how I responded to what I was feeling.

Post-Traumatic Stress

One of the most disturbing things for me was the trauma. My heart would begin to pound whenever I heard a siren. We had had to call the ambulance three times, including the day before John died. I had horrible olfactory flashbacks of John's last night, and the sound of his rattling breath would become loud in my ears. Finally, my friend Margaret, a Virtues Project master facilitator, called me to ask "How are you, really?" I began to describe in detail everything about that last night. When I would stop, thinking this was too horrible for her to hear, she said, "Tell me everything." When I had completely emptied my cup, she said, "Linda, you were so faithful in caring for John." Then she repeated what a friend had told her about grief: "It's like an amputation. You never get over it. You get used to it." Her companioning was an incredible gift. I never had another flashback after that.

The Need for Space

One night I agreed to be one of the authors to do a reading for a charitable fund-raising event. I read a passage from *The Family Virtues Guide*. One of the other writers came up to me afterwards and asked me how I was. I said, "I'm sad. I'm navigating the waves." He smiled gently and said, "What could be better than to be sad at a time like this?" He told me how utterly bereft he was when his mother died. Then, he said, "You'll need a lot of space to get through the grief. When you think you have all the space you need, double it." He understood so well, and he was right. It takes a huge amount of energy to face and heal through the grieving process and we cannot simply resume all of our normal responsibilities without paying a huge price.

Identity Theft

When we lose someone who is central in our lives, we lose a huge part of ourselves. Who are we without our couple-ness, our other half, our best friend? Without the one who was our story-keeper, our mirror? It feels as though a harsh spiritual winter has descended, with its cold, colorless emptiness. There is a quiet part of us that knows this too shall pass. When winter comes, we need to trust that spring will come again.

Private Mourning

It is really helpful to shed healing tears. Go to a private space where no one will interrupt you, lie on your bed or the floor on comfortable pillows. Make a sound that reflects how you feel inside. Not everyone can get to their tears, but this may help you to do so. Some find that the privacy of their car and seeing something they enjoyed with the departed helps to release emotions. Lovingly give yourself an opportunity to get to your deepest feelings.

The Rhythm of Healing

Years ago, when I was a psycho-therapist working with suicidal people and those who were deeply traumatized, as well as in my hospice work with the dying, I learned a wonderful secret. It was a way to face the inevitable floodtide of emotions that well up in anticipatory grief as well as in bereavement after a death.

The most healing approach to grief at any stage is two-fold. Just as a tide ebbs and flows, we need to find safe outlets for our tears, our anger, and all the facets of our grief. We need to let it out. Just as importantly, we need to take a break, get our minds off the grief, do something that brings us pleasure, or literally get away. Watch a movie, go out for lunch, have a new adventure, spend time laughing with a friend. Go into the grief deeply, then come up for air. We need to repeat this ebb and flow process until we notice a steady, gentler current.

I have always companioned people in grief to help them get to the heart of the matter – the guts of the pain – then guide their attention to something they are looking forward to, something joyful or fun. This method served me well in my own time of sorrow.

"Tears are the best cleanser."
Evelyn Belzer, my oldest friend

SUSTAINING VIRTUES:

Patience is quiet hope and faith that things will turn out right. We trust the process of life. Patience is a balm to one who is grieving. It gives us hope.

Hope is looking to the future with trust and faith. Without hope, we lose our will to live fully. Hope gives us the courage to keep moving forward. It sustains our souls.

siblings had lost both their parents in close proximity, nothing was ever said. All of them developed ulcers. They simply couldn't stomach their loss and had no safe outlet for releasing their pain. So it ate away at them.

I've Got You Under My Skin

Some people get welts or rashes. My son Chris experienced an outbreak of eczema on the inner part of both arms when unable to see his children for a period of months. He had been striving to connect with them, but had been prevented. When he was visiting some Maori healers in New Zealand, one of them saw the eczema and said, "Ahh! You miss holding your children in your arms." He tried all kinds of balms and treatments, but only when he was able to once again embrace his children, did it clear up completely.

Back Pain

Lower back pain is a common ailment during bereavement. According to Louise Hay it signifies the loss of support. The ones who "have our backs" have disappeared. My brother Tommy had terrible back pain after John's death. He felt the loss of his twin and best friend deeply but had difficulty expressing tears. He had to sleep on the floor for a while until it subsided.

Jolene, a friend who has a full schedule of community service and organizing had invited her mother to visit her for several months and was looking forward to having quality time with her. Three weeks before she was due to arrive, her mother had a massive stroke and died.

Jolene was preparing a large party to celebrate her 50th birthday and encouraged by her husband, went ahead with it. She then organized a large women's conference and went ahead with other commitments, soldiering through them all. She began to experience excruciating back pain, and an MRI showed three cracks in her lower spine and a leak of spinal fluid which had calcified in the form of what her surgeon called "an arrow". One might say her deferred grief stabbed her in the back. Once surgery was performed, she was able to walk without pain. She confessed to me that she wonders how it might have gone differently if she had taken the time to recognize and release her sorrow.

Sleep Disorders

I wasn't able to sleep well for weeks before John passed, and then afterwards, the sleeplessness continued. This adds to the fatigue and exhaustion that are a natural part of grief. Some people have the opposite reaction and sleep for hours during the day as well as at night. Others find that they just feel sluggish for months and that sleep is broken. I feel it wise to get a non-addictive sleep aide from a homeopath or physician to help us through this time.

Heartbreak

A journalist told me that the expressions people have come up with for grief are truly apt: "Gut wrenching", "bowled over", "heartbroken". She discovered this when her own beloved mother died. I found that "heartache" is a literal state that did not leave me for many months following John's passing.

One thing that bothers me is when grief is medicalized – when grief is mistaken for depression. It is a totally different animal even if it looks like the same emotions. It is a natural process, not a form of pathology or a mental disorder! Therefore, in my view, it should not be medicated away!

We were in Australia during a deadly flood, when many tragedies occurred for people living near rivers in Queensland. One story the newscasters kept repeating was about a four year old literally swept out of her mother's arms by the raging torrent. They showed an outback sheep farmer with a reporter who asked him how he would deal with the tragedy: "Croy, croy, croy, hug somebody, even a bloke. It don't matter."

When in the throes of the grief, we need to have great compassion for our own bodies and our emotions, and care for them tenderly.

"When he spoke, what tender words he used!
So softly, that like flakes of feathered snow,
they melted as they fell."
John Dryden, poet

SUSTAINING VIRTUES:

Honesty allows us to be open and transparent, whatever we are feeling or experiencing. We are able to be fully ourselves.

Understanding is having clear insight into ideas and feelings. We thoughtfully seek to comprehend the full truth. We are deeply present to others with compassion and accuracy, helping them to discern their own clarity.

HEALING STEPS:

1. Be mindful that your body may well be affected by your grief. Take care of yourself with tenderness and patience. Eat. Sleep. Exercise. Talk and cry.

2. Do your best to have safe outlets for your emotions in order to minimize the physical impact of your grief.

32 OUT OF MY MIND

"The grief and sadness fill up our heart and mind, leaving little room to process other information."
www.elderthink.com

A significant loss can tilt our world on its axis. When grief hits us, it absorbs so much of our energy that it short-circuits our normal capacities to be, think, and do. One of the strangest manifestations of grief after a traumatic loss comes in the form of mental lapses, such as extreme forgetfulness or beliefs that haunt us, whether they make realistic sense or not.

Shock and Awe
There is an initial shock after a death. The truth of it is just unbelievable. How can this person we love be breathing one moment and not the next? How can that life be over? A sense of shock is particularly overwhelming after a sudden death.

In her soul stirring memoir, The Year of Magical Thinking, author Joan Didion describes how grief affected her after her husband's sudden fatal heart attack. He died in the middle of a sentence as she was preparing lunch in the next room. They were both authors, working at home in their New York apartment and spent most of their time together each day.

For months, she kept imagining that she saw her husband on the streets of New York. She refused to give his shoes away because of the persistent thought that he would come back and need them again. "I know why we try to keep the dead alive: we try to keep them with us," she wrote.

My neighbour, George, wouldn't leave the house for months, because "Eunice might come back." His children worried about his mental state, but it seemed to me just an understandable resistance to believing she was really gone. To me, this aspect of grief is not something for which to see a psychiatrist. We just have to find our way through it, hopefully with the help of compassionate listeners.

Mind Like a Steel Sieve

As grief sucks up our available energy, including our mental acuity, it can leave us wondering if we will ever emerge from the morass. It has mind-dulling effects, including major collateral damage to memory.

Several months after John's death, Dan and I had planned a special evening of dinner with friends and a concert Dan was especially eager to attend. It was a rare appearance by folk singer Leon Bibb, then in his eighties. I had a very full day with two meetings, and found I didn't have time to go home and change, so I arranged with Dan to come in our second car. I picked up the tickets to save time, and rushed to the restaurant. Dan seemed preoccupied, and I sat there wondering why he seemed antsy to leave right after dinner and felt he was being a bit rude to our friends. Afterwards, the tickets secure in my purse, I drove directly home from the restaurant. A half hour later, I began to panic about why Dan had not followed me. I drove out in the rain looking for his car, expecting to find him in a ditch! As he pulled up beside me, he said, "I guess you decided to skip the concert." I was horrified. This special event we had been looking forward to for weeks had utterly vacated my mind!

When I shared this experience with Jackie, a friend whose husband had died of brain cancer, she said she made a wrong turn in a town she had known well for years. "Suddenly I felt completely lost. I panicked, and had to sit and quiet my heart, and study a map to get my bearings." Grief literally disorients us.

The week approaching the first anniversary of John's death, I was a wreck. The beautiful personalized headstone we designed with such love was still not placed on his grave, as there had been drainage problems in the cemetery. John still had an unmarked grave and I felt devastated about it. Finally, just before the date of his anniversary, it was done.

That week, in the midst of my angst, a mental lapse occurred that still makes me shudder. For months, I had been scheduled to be on an international radio show out of the U.S., live, for a one hour phone interview. I spoke with the producer the day before, and felt I was ready. The morning of the show, I slept right through it. I had a horrible haunting feeling that whole day that something was amiss but couldn't pinpoint it. Finally, I got an email from the host of the show, asking courteously why I hadn't answered their several calls the day of the broadcast. She had gone on to do the program herself, reading passages from my books and talking with the radio audience. Since it was a live show, they couldn't get another author to fill in. I was mortified! What a shock to "forget" something that important! The intensified grief of that week erased everything else from my mind. Fortunately, the host was kind enough to trust me to make amends by having me on the show a couple of weeks later. You can believe I had signs all over the house and my office with alarms galore!

The Energy Vampire

A common experience in grieving is a sense of enervating fatigue, low energy that can persist for weeks or months. Deep emotions take a physical toll, and grief perhaps most of all. As I've said, I consider this very different from depression. It is natural sadness, and it is perfectly healthy to go through a period like this. Journaling the question, "How am I today?", can be helpful, in observing our journey through grief, noticing the small shifts. We also need to remember to balance our attention, stepping out of our grief into enjoyable activities from time to time.

Dr. Nancy Reeves, a psychologist who specializes in grief recovery, has a helpful model of the energy shifts in the grieving process in her book, A Path Through Loss. This diagram illustrates the changes most people experience in the amount of energy taken up by grief, then survival, and finally, by life enhancement once again. Nancy says, "Grievers go at their own pace through the circles depending on the implications and meanings they are grieving. When a new implication arises, they may return to an earlier circle as they are using more energy to deal with the concern."

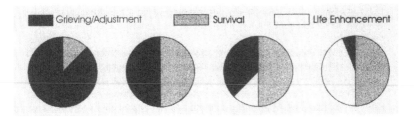

This is a hopeful, and in my experience, accurate model of the process.

> *"I awoke to the confusion of a new day...*
> *What to make order of? What to let go?*
> *...I think I will go down to the river and just watch it flow.*
> *It's been a long time since I have done something really important."*
> David Sluyter, author

SUSTAINING VIRTUES:

Forbearance is patience, fortitude and acceptance under trying circumstances. We tolerate hardship with good grace. We quietly call on our self-restraint. We are long-suffering in situations that we cannot control. We do not allow the trials of life to steal our joy.

Orderliness - We create an environment of peace and order. We plan step by step instead of going in circles. This virtue can help us in the midst of the chaos of losing our normal bearings in the grief process.

HEALING STEPS:

1. Be patient and compassionate with yourself, as you would with any wounded person, knowing that grief takes time and energy.

2. Don't expect to be at your normal level of productivity until you are ready. It just won't work. Carve out as much

space as you can afford and refrain from taking on any responsibilities you can postpone.

3. Use your orderliness to make lists. Put everything you have to do on a calendar and/or smart phone. Look at your calendar before you go to sleep and when you wake up. Set alarms.

33 A CRISIS OF FAITH

"Wherever there is ruin, there is hope for treasure. Why do you not
seek the treasure of God in the wasted heart?"
Jalal'u'din Rumi, Sufi mystic poet

I never dreamed it could happen to me. Not only did my faith
waver during the last ten days of John's life, when he was in
excruciating pain, but after he died as well. I felt utterly lost, bereft
not only of John but also of God.

I have believed in God all my life, in the eternal life of the soul, the
afterlife, and the transformative power of tests. I had experienced
Divine guidance more times than I could remember and had a rich
prayer life. Faith defined me.

In the many years of my daily meditation practice, I have been
blessed by visions and visits, which often come out of the blue. One
day about two weeks before John's death, I prayed my emotional
and physical exhaustion. I said aloud, "I can't keep this up. I can't
breathe." I felt a holy figure standing before me, breathing into me.
That tender Presence gave me strength for the last days. Then, I
heard, "Everything you do for John, you do for Me." It was the balm
I needed to persevere.

A few days before John's death, I was astonished during my private
reflection time to hear the words, "We are letting you down gently."
"You're letting me down gently?" I was amazed at this expression of
Grace, assuming John's dying was all about him, but of course it is
about the ones left behind too. And for me, it was gentle. I wanted
nothing more that day than for John to be released from his mortal
pain and limitations.

Faith was at the core of my relationships, my writing, my work, and
my sense of meaning. Yet, as the grief of bereavement took me over,
it didn't seem to make an iota of difference in alleviating my grief
and anxiety. How could this be? I felt disconnected from my own

soul, as if it had been hollowed out and, having lost its substance, just drifted away. It was not an intellectual change born of thought, but a visceral, disorienting reaction.

The Sacred Wound

Despite my exquisite experiences of faithful, intimate support from the spiritual realm, the loss of John opened my oldest wound – abandonment. For me, in this painful journey of grief, abandonment trumped faith. This old tormenting emotion of mine was what American poet Robert Bly calls "the long bag we drag behind us," of repressed emotions – our dark shadow self.

In his book, Soulcraft, Bill Plotkin writes of the sacred wound that is both our nemesis and our greatest portal to spiritual growth. It is redemptive to discern the treasures found only in exploring our deepest wound.

Early emotional rejection and abandonment was mine, threatening my sense of worth, my personhood. It was also the catalyst for the deep compassion I have for the suffering of others. It led me to a career in social work, psychotherapy, suicide prevention, community healing and eventually to founding The Virtues Project. I didn't want any child to suffer from the cataclysmic loss of self-esteem resulting from the guilt-laden, shaming parenting common in my parents' generation.

I thought my bag of pain was long gone. My life was filled by a loving marriage, my joyful kinship with John, many soul friends, my closeness to my sons, a spiritual community I loved, and work I adored. But when John was in pain in his final days, the oldest scar in my heart began to rupture and bleed. I felt helpless, terrified, and once again, deserted.

Reunion

When John died, at first I was elated at his escape from his body, believing that he was in the next world, enjoying a new life of joy and freedom from pain. About ten days later, an upwelling of grief

HEALING STEPS:

1. Sit with your grief. Hold it gently. Be present to your own experience. Don't resist it. Let it wash over you. Don't retreat into cynicism, victimhood or self-pity. Let clean compassion immerse you as you release your tears.

2. Pray the real. Pray your flatness, your loneliness, your feelings of desertion. Open yourself to the Divine response.

3. Have faith in the resilience of faith, even when it seems to desert you. This too shall pass.

34 HOW LONG, OH LORD?

"How long, O Lord? Will you forget me forever?
How long will you hide your face from me?
How long must I take counsel in my soul and have sorrow in my
heart all the day?"
Psalm 13

When we are in the throes of grief after a death, we wonder how long it will go on. It is so unpredictable. We are hit by a huge wave of it and then find ourselves in calmer waters. We begin to focus more on our everyday life than obsessing about the one we have lost, when suddenly, we fall into another whirling vortex of sorrow. No one can tell us how long it will take, simply because it's different for each of us. The time it takes to heal in the journey of grief depends on several factors.

How Close We Were
First and foremost is the depth of the relationship with the person who has died, and how central he or she has been in our lives. If that individual was our center of gravity, the size of the space carved out by our grief reflects that. If our lives were entwined, as is often the case with a spouse, a best friend, our child, parent, or sibling, we are left with a hole in our soul. It can take years to heal rather than months.

John was my oldest and in many ways, my closest friend. I had been his mentor and protector throughout our lives, and he had been mine. We had been each other's daily "story-keepers" since he moved back to Salt Spring after his last Disney project in Japan. And because I was his primary caregiver, our closeness deepened even more.

Survivor Guilt
My neighbor George, who lost his wife after 64 years of marriage, told me, "It's been three years and I'm just beginning to accept that she is gone." He was resisting his children's invitation to go on a

at the surface, and trust that we will not drown.

There are three basic phases of grief:

First, the period when grief takes up a huge amount of our energy, typically for a period of many weeks or months.

Second, our energy begins to mobilize around survival strategies, which help us get through the grief. Things like finding a compassionate listener, doing rituals, taking time to cry or vent, journaling, and establishing a routine for eating and sleeping.

Third, we begin to enjoy life again, little by little and day by day. We reconnect with life, focus on work, friendship, activities that are life enhancing and engaging. Instead of grief being triggered when we think of our loved one, we begin to enjoy our memories. As my mother in law said, after losing two of her children to cancer within seven weeks, "Death is final, but memories last for life."

"In time the loss becomes a memory instead of a presence."
www.elderthink.com/memory

SUSTAINING VIRTUES:

Patience is waiting peacefully. It is quiet hope and faith that things will turn out right. You will get through this.

Resilience is the strength of spirit to recover from adversity. We overcome obstacles by tapping into a deep well of faith and endurance.

HEALING STEPS:

1. The sooner we accept and befriend our own grief, rather than judging it or letting anyone else's judgment get to us, the gentler will be the process of healing.

2. We need to call on our courage and trust to believe that we can rebound as the grief subsides. As it does, we need to detach from guilt about letting go of our sadness, as if it is a way of being loyal to our loved one. Isn`t a happy life what our loved one would want for us?

3. As we resume a life of fullness and pleasures without our loved one, let us simply be grateful.

35 RITUALS

*"I will not forget you! See, I have engraved you
on the palms of my hands."*
Isaiah 49

My father died the year after John, Dan and I first moved to Salt Spring Island in British Columbia and started working together on the idea which later blossomed into The Virtues Project.

One day as I was walking through the living room, an inner voice gave me a warning. "Prepare yourself. Something is going to happen." Later that day we heard that my father had collapsed on his way to speak at a conference in Tennessee and was in hospital there, very close to death.

We immediately flew to be with him. John remained behind to help tend to my father until his passing a few weeks later, and when he returned home, he brought with him the long, plush bathrobe, which Dad had worn until the end of his life. It was deep blue with a southwest design. John began to wear it in the morning when we shared breakfast and prayers together. Then one morning, I noticed it hanging in my closet. For at least a year, we would each wear it for a while, then slip it into the other's bedroom closet. It wrapped us in comfort. We never said a word about it, which somehow felt more reverent.

There are many ways to create personal rituals and ceremonies beyond the funeral that many families hold, which may help you to heal through the grieving process.

Shrining

It is common for one who is grieving to place photographs of the beloved around their home, and to do other things to honour their memory. Our neighbour, George, placed a lovely cloth and a flower in the lounger beside his own, where his departed wife Eunice always sat. Before he went to bed each night he would kiss her picture and talk with her. Then, he decided to begin sleeping in her twin bed, instead of his own, just to feel "closer".

I still have photos of John's beautiful face throughout our home. Before he died, he bought me an uncharacteristically sentimental gift, a painting of an angel, with the words "There's an angel watching over you." I have it above the sink with a photo of the two of us.

Create Sacred Space

When you feel ready, it can be very healing to set aside a special time for remembering. Light candles, get quiet and reverent, and put on some music that reminds you of your loved one. Spread a cloth on a table. Take out photographs, videos, audiotapes, cards, letters and memorabilia that remind you of your loved one, and place them on a table in front of you. Watch the videos. Listen to recordings. Let the memories enfold you. To be honest, it took me months to get ready to hear recordings of John's voice, including his last lectures. When I did, it gently cracked open the unhealed feelings that I had unwittingly kept inside. I wept and laughed through it. It was time.

Listen to Music

One way to help you get to your healing tears is to play music that reminds you of your loved one. John left behind an extensive CD collection, which I have shared with other family members, and his I-Pod. I find it deeply comforting to listen to the jazz, classical and other music we enjoyed listening to together. If you and your departed partner had your own love song, listen to it and let the tears flow.

Remembrance Story-Telling Circles

Share a meal and memories with others who cared for the one who has died. This is not a time to excavate anger or disappointments. Focus on the humorous things, the gifts and virtues of the person's life, the sweet legacy of the happier memories.

36 IN YOUR MEMORY

"When I come to the end of the road
And the sun has set for me
I want no rites in a gloom-filled room.
Why cry for a soul set free?
Miss me a little – but not too long
And not with your head bowed low.
Remember the love that we once shared.
Miss me – but let me go.
For this is a journey that we all must take
And each must go alone. It's all a part of the Master's plan
A step on the road to home.
When you are lonely and sick of heart
Go to the friends we know
And bury your sorrows in doing good deeds.
Miss me – but let me go! "

This poem was found in the pocket of a dead British soldier in
World War I. The author is unknown. "Bury your sorrows in doing
good deeds", says the poet.

One of the most powerful ways to heal the pain of grief is to do a
service in the name of our loved one. It can be a small kindness or a
big event, a charitable donation or even a new career. Some sacred
writings say that when we pray for the departed and do things
in their name, it accrues to their souls. Pouring our sorrow into
service is alchemical. It transforms it and makes it more bearable.

The Balm of Dedication
In the year after John's death, Dan and I gradually got back to
work. We dedicated every conference presentation or retreat event
to John's memory. At the start of each power point, I placed a
dedication slide with John's photo and the dates of his life. When I
would bring soup to a sick friend, or visited someone in hospital,
I would silently do it in John's memory. These practices were and
continue to be, deeply comforting.

I saw a child on Oprah Winfrey's television show who found this to be the only way to heal his profound grief after the death of his twin brother Eric. Twelve year old Aaron was utterly bereft after his brother died of brain cancer when they were nine. From the time they were born, they had been inseparable best friends. Their mother said that in the sonogram taken of them in the womb, "they were holding hands." Aaron appeared on Oprah's show with Nate Berkus, who was helping Aaron with a business enterprise. Little did Nate know it would become a healing connection for them both. As mentioned earlier, Nate's partner Fernando had been killed in a tsunami while they were on holiday in Thailand.

After Eric's death, Aaron's grieving parents Angela and Jeff were terrified when he said he didn't want to be here anymore. His teachers reported that all he did was stare out the window and cry. "It didn't feel like life," Aaron told Oprah. "It felt like I was just there." Desperate for help, Angela and Jeff called their family pediatrician, Dr. Corder. She could barely recognize Aaron, he had changed so much. "What do you like to do?" she asked him. He said, "I like to cook," and she said, "Okay, we're gonna cook for your brother." She gave him $20 and told him she was his first investor. On the way home, Aaron and his mother stopped at a grocery store to buy ingredients. For the first time in ages, he was smiling.

Aaron poured his excellence and creativity into baking cookies. He named his company "DoughJangles". He said, "You have to do something. I do this for him." Aaron says he thinks about his brother with every cookie he makes. "I think he would be proud of me," he says. "I think he'd be happy that I didn't just give up." On the show, Oprah introduced Aaron to one of his idols, Chef Paula Deen, who told him, "Live your life as a tribute to your brother. Celebrate his life through yours." (www.oprah.com/oprahshow/Nate-Helps-a-Family-with-Grief)

Donate What You Can
Dan and I contributed to the Cancer Society and Caring Bridge in John's name. We held a huge sale of John's belongings and

contributed most of the proceeds to the Haiti earthquake relief fund. Friends donated to other causes in his memory, and whenever we received a note telling us this, we felt comforted.

Aaron donates a portion of his DoughJangles revenues to charity. "It made me feel good about myself to donate to the charities that helped my brother," he said.

Some families donate a bench or some other public gifting in the name of their loved one. Then they go and sit there to remember them.

Do Something
After I was divorced and remarried, my teenage sons went to live with their father in Florida for an undetermined time. They were far across the country from where Dan and I lived in Oregon, and I didn't hear from them unless I called. I went into a deep depression. Then, something pulled me out of it. Our faith community announced the need for volunteers to help the Hmong refugees in Portland, and something stirred inside me. I began volunteering to help them find housing and jobs. I was too busy focusing on their needs to wallow in my own depression. These lovely newcomers helped me at least as much as I helped them.

The helplessness that accompanies grief can dissipate when we take some action – any positive action – that honors the memory of our loved one.

"We've learned that honoring our son's memory with our daily actions and never forgetting him are the most important parts of the coping process."
Joe Sterling, New York Times article

SUSTAINING VIRTUES:

Charity – Charity springs from compassion for the suffering of others. It moves us to respond to their needs, giving help and kindness. We make a genuine difference in their lives.

Initiative is the springboard of our creativity. We dare to be original. We use our creativity to bring something new into the world.

HEALING STEPS:

1. Think of something you like to do. Do it in the name of your loved one.

2. Pray for the soul of your loved one and spend time doing kindnesses in their memory.

3. Contribute as you can to a worthwhile cause that captures your enthusiasm and compassion.

37 GETTING AWAY

"I'm not running away from my responsibilities. I'm running to them.
There's nothing negative about running away to save my life."
Joseph Heller, author

John died in July. As the executor of his estate, it took me a full six months, with Dan's orderly and constant assistance and that of our lawyer, to deal with the bulk of the legalities and John's accumulated papers and belongings. He often said, "Lin, I'm so sorry to leave you with all this," gazing around his large house full of "stuff". The work of caring for him, and the daily discipline of containing my own grief so I would not be imposing it on him, took every ounce of my energy. I desperately needed something to look forward to when it was over.

Create an LFT
Dan and I talked about a "looking forward to" plan, and it became my lifeline of hope during the arduous days before and after John's passing. We planned a trip to the South Pacific – our beloved Cook Islands, where I had started my book, A Pace of Grace, and where we had returned several times to teach The Virtues Project. The promise of that trip sustained us.

I wrote in my journal:
Like birth, death is messy, and grief is messier still. I crave clear, clean space around me, and I'm dealing with piles and piles of stuff, and papers and legalities. Our trip away is a balm I look forward to.

My friend, Susanne, whose husband also died of Glio Blastoma the same month as John did, planned a trip to Florida to visit her daughter and baby granddaughter.

Jackie and Doug had been sailors, and she went on a chartered sailing ship after he died, which was perfect as her LFT. She didn't have to cook, had no responsibility, yet she was on the sea again, which they had loved. She had people to talk to if she chose, but could also be alone. Her secret to creating solitude on board, she told me when she got back, was to sit with a sketch book, and people would leave her to it.

A nurse told me of a man who visited his wife every night for weeks. She said to him, "You are so loyal. How do you keep it up? What keeps you going?" He reached into his jacket and pulled out an open ticket to Hawaii. He said, "As soon as she goes, I'm on the plane."

Escape the Triggers
When you are in a house or a community where everything you see and do reminds you of the one who is gone, it continually reopens the wound of grief. There was a small sushi restaurant where John and I often lunched, and I couldn't go in for months. We had become friends with the Korean couple who ran it, who called themselves Ben and Joanne. John had been stationed in Korea in the army, and knew some Korean phrases, which he spoke with them. They adored him, and when he died I went in to give them a gift of some Korean tiger sculptures John loved. Joanna came out from the counter and wept in my arms. I simply knew I couldn't look into her face for a while without sobbing. All it takes for tears to come is one glance of compassion.

Therapeutic Change
They say don't make any big moves or changes until a year after a significant death. However, I found that a total change of scene was just what I needed as a reprieve from grief. After doing a brief service project in Rarotonga, Dan and I escaped to the solitude of Aitutaki, a beautiful outer island in the Cooks. I spent hours in a hammock beneath a swaying palm, just staring, then sleeping, reading, then swimming. Dan happily gazed out at the water from our deck, watching the sea birds fly by. There were baby chicks wandering around the bungalows and when I came in for a drink, there sat Dan with a baby chick perched on his knee.

My friend Pat needed to move out of the marital bedroom after

38 COMING HOME

"Broken heart, you timeless wonder. What a small place to be."
Michael Ondaatje, *The Cat's Table*

When one takes time away, it can be quietly healing. Then there is
the return home. Familiar surroundings that remind us of the one
who has died reopen the wounds of grief. We can only let it be what
it is – yet another opportunity to ride the waves.

Find Your Balance

The more central the departed person was in one's life, the bigger
the adjustment to life without them. Whatever space that person
held in our lives is now a gaping, empty hole. And one is reluctant
to fill it. Going away helped me to detach for a while, yet in coming
home, I found my grief lying in wait. I had to call on a deep well
of patience and compassion for myself. I would often cry when
I was driving alone, and I continued to see my grief counsellor. I
found the Grief Recovery Group run by Hospice a safe place to
express the truth, which most people didn't seem able to cope with.
If I honestly told them how I was, they would look puzzled as if
thinking, why is this taking you so long?

Two years after John's passing, someone asked me an interesting
question: "Have you accepted his death?" "What does that even
mean?" I wondered. But I knew that the truthful answer was no.
The surreal feeling about his death persisted – a huge "WHAT??!!"
deep in my mind. How could this have happened? How could
this vital life be over, this cherished voice be stilled? Part of the
homecoming for me after my peaceful sojourn on warm beaches
was to face this – to accept my lingering unacceptance. Does one
ever completely accept the unacceptable?

In speaking with others who had lost people they loved deeply I
found this sense of unreality to be a common experience.

Yet, as many people are quick to tell you, life must go on. It is essential to keep in mind the need to balance our attention between compassionately tending to our sorrow, and then focusing on what is life-giving and enjoyable to us. Bring your attention in and bring it out. Like breathing.

Reengage

My grief in the first year or so felt like a constant current, a silent river of tears moving just below the surface of awareness. For months, I felt this presence of sorrow, as a hollow emptiness at my core. I thought about John constantly. I needed pictures of him everywhere.

When my friend Jackie came home from one of her trips away in the second year after her husband's death, she felt out of sorts. "Where's my buddy?" she would say. It's one thing to be off on an adventure meeting new people, but coming home was still hard. I wondered if she would stay.

So, what do we do? We simply can't go back to life as it was, because it is different now. Most of us have responsibilities and other relationships that need our attention, and life simply demands that we rise to the needs around us. For some, like Wendy, who works as a cashier at a local pharmacy, her job was her salvation. After her son's suicide during a terminal illness, work was a ladder of normalcy with which to climb out of the hole of despair.

I have found that in the face of a major change, before I can discern how to renew my life, I need to clear a space for it. Letting go of what no longer fits our lives is a deeply cleansing process, and opens us to the new.

Create a Space of Grace

Even when the change is a tragic one, it presents us with an opportunity to recreate our lives – to change our colors, to rearrange our living space, to replace old habits, to decide how we want to spend this one precious life.

In the months before John died, Dan would go home to our house down the road and paint. He repainted the walls of each room in colours John had helped us pick out, and then he started on the outside. He refreshed our home from top to bottom. After John's death, he deconstructed all the decks and rebuilt them. He designed lovely built-in flower boxes for my spring tulips.

Once we moved out of John's house, and were back in our own home, with its freshly painted walls, I needed to clean. I cleared years of accumulated files, hauled reams of paper to the recycling depot. Let go of old clothes and old stuff while changing out of old roles.

In the face of death, one of the gifts is to realize that each of us is going to die, for real. It ignites a new flame of deep appreciation for living, and an inner urge to make the most of the time we have left. One way to do that is to make a commitment to live fully once again. This can be a generative time of re-creation.

"The real voyage of discovery consists not in seeking new landscapes, but in having new eyes."
Marcel Proust, French author

SUSTAINING VIRTUES:

Commitment is the strength to go the distance. We dare to care once again about our lives, ourselves. Once we discern a direction, we go for it wholeheartedly. We don't hold back, second-guess our decision or hesitate to act on it fully. We set goals and achieve them. We make promises and keep them. Commitment deepens our capacity to carry responsibility with grace.

Peacefulness is inner calm and tranquility. Inner peace comes from quiet reflection and prayer. We release the past and let anxiety go. We keep a graceful pace, not allowing ourselves to be rushed or overwhelmed. We find ways to be tranquil.

HEALING STEPS:

1. When you come home, be tender with yourself. Recognize that grief will be triggered by the familiar, and let it be.

2. Remember to put one foot in grief and one foot in hope so that you can stand on your own holy ground.

3. As you re-enter the world of work and family and other responsibilities, set aside space in which you can to tend to the wounds of grief. Be really patient.

VIII REINVENTING YOURSELF

"Let the beauty we love be what we do. There are hundreds of ways to kneel and kiss the ground."
Jalal'u'din Rumi, Sufi mystic poet

As we live through the first years after the death of one we love, how can we renew our own life, now so changed? How do we befriend the lingering grief? The question of identity arises -- who am I now? And we must hold this question with great patience and mindfulness.

How do we claim the gifts of our grief? How do we get to the other side to receive its blessings?

With every loss comes new freedom. Our response to it determines the quality of our lives from this point on. It's not just a question of survival, but of design and recreation. For better or for worse, this time of healing brings with it a fresh opportunity to start over. What we make of it will set a new course for the rest of our lives.

39 A YEAR OF FIRSTS

"You can clutch the past so tightly to your chest
that it leaves your arms too full to embrace the present."
Jan Glidewell, journalist

I think of the first year after loss as a bridging time, in which one
slowly and gently crosses from "the way we were" to a new existence.
For me, bereavement in all its forms was utterly surprising. As a
person of faith, I simply didn't expect to feel it so deeply and to have
it affect my life so profoundly.

An Unfamiliar World

One of the surprises grief held for me in the year following John's
death was how disorienting and at times frightening it was to
attempt things alone that we had done together. John was my
constant social companion, giving Dan the space for his more
reclusive way of being.

I remember standing at the verge of the huge field where our
island community holds Fall Fair each year, acutely aware I would
be going in without John. I paused, and felt my heart thudding. It
triggered a memory of walking through the fair with John, greeting
our friends, eating corn on the cob, and helping tote plates to the
dish-washing booth our Baha'i community ran. My chest tightened
with what was becoming a familiar angst. I took a breath and
stepped over the edge of the field. It felt absurdly courageous. I
wrote in my journal the next morning:

Today nearly eight weeks after John's death, I feel drained, literally
had the runs. I am awash in tears. I faced the first time at Fall Fair
without him. "This is a year of firsts," a friend said, "and then you'll
have a year of seconds, and one of thirds..."

When my friend Pat's husband David died at ninety-two, she was
eighty-eight. They had been married for sixty-seven years. After
the funeral she was invited to visit with relatives for a while – a

fully experience our senses. We refuse to rush. Living mindfully lightens our lives by helping us to detach from our emotions. We transform anger to justice. We seek joy instead of mere desire. We cultivate our inner vision, aware of life's lessons as they unfold. Mindfulness brings us serenity.

Confidence is having faith in oneself and in life. We feel capable and competent. We trust that we have the strength to cope with whatever happens. Confidence helps us to be free of worry. It brings the strength to try new things, to gain mastery through practice. With confidence, we cast off self-limiting beliefs and doubts. We offer our gifts as a worthy contribution. When opportunity comes, we step up to it. We just say "yes".

HEALING STEPS:

1. Mindfully find your balance between retreating and stepping out, giving yourself the space for solitude and reaching out to connect with others.

2. Summon your courage and trust that you will regain your confidence as you take step after step on this unfamiliar track of going it alone, without the one you love.

40 THE COMFORT OF CREATIVITY

"Come with me and you'll be in a world of pure imagination...
If you want to view paradise simply look around and view it.
Anything you want to, do it."
Leslie Bricusse and Anthony Newley
(from Willy Wonka & the Chocolate Factory)

It is said that our emotions and our creativity abide in the same part of our brains. Perhaps that is one reason it is healing to express grief in some artistic way. Whether poetry, music, weaving, sculpture or painting, try your hand at it. You may be surprised at how helpful it is in bringing deeper realities to light.

Find Your Creative Portal

My friend Susanne, blogged about a painting she had done in the aftermath of her husband's death from brain cancer. She is a writer, not a painter, yet found, through the help of an occupational therapist, that putting color to canvas was a powerful release. She included a photo of her painting, which contained slashes of red and black over a few other colors. She entitled it "Give Anger a Voice."

One man began to build things, to pound nails, to sand and polish wood. He found that it absorbed his grief and gave him deep satisfaction. He thought of each chest or table as a gift to his wife.

Soul Collage

Each summer I take a retreat with nine soul sisters. We always do crafts. Kara and Cheryll, who came with Kara's cello the last night of John's life, taught our group the art of SoulCollage. I found it immensely helpful in venting strong emotions during the months after John died. You find magazine pictures – not words, only images – that express what you feel, and can piece them together and glue them onto a 5 X 8 card. Then, you write on the back the date and "I am the one who..." www.soulcollage.com

I created my first cards at our retreat the month after John passed.

During my turn in our sharing circle, in which I shed copious tears, I felt the love and compassion of my sisters companioning me in my pain. Then, I spent hours in silence, choosing images.

My first collage was of a padded chaise longue on the deck of a beachside bungalow. I found a pair of white slippers to paste in, and palm trees – an homage to Dan's and my LFT ("looking forward to") in the Cook Islands of the South Pacific planned for the following winter. I wrote on the back, "I am the one, exhausted by love and loss, needing deep rest."

My second was of a dancer, seated on the floor, one arm leaning on her knee, her head resting on her arm, looking contemplative. "I am the one who is contemplating the next steps in the dance."

Give Words to Your Experience
Those who facilitate grief recovery at hospice often recommend journaling, as a way of giving voice both to grief and what is helping one navigate it. This can be in the form of narrative, just simple phrases, responding to the question, "How am I really?" or "How am I now?" It can include sketches or pictures from magazines that resonate, or poetry.

One afternoon, a few weeks after John died, I was resting in a reclining chair in our garden, staring up at the swaying branches of a tall pine, feeling a deep bittersweet contentment. I had my journal and pen beside me. I wrote the following poem:

SOLITUDE
I nurse at the breast of solitude
the sweetness of silence in my own company
a solace
in the space I have cleared for breath.

Distancing from detritus, demands, distractions, deadlines and desk,
my will wavers,
needs the time to consider carefully

what the yeses of my new life will reveal.

Even friendship is an intrusion
at a time such as this.
I crave tranquillity of thought,
freed, detached from daily expectations.

This new pace of grace
rhythm of my heart
surrenders to grief,
bends in its gusts,
just is what it is.
I feed contentedly.

Before and After
Months later, as my grief surged in waves, I felt the need to create a new soul collage. I happened upon a magazine photo of a gigantic wave, about to engulf an unaware surfer standing casually on his board. "I am the one who is overwhelmed by surging grief, taken unawares." As that phase shifted, I created another collage with a photo of a dancer in full leap, placed above gentle waves. I found the dancer on a program of the Alvin Ailey Ballet I attended with a friend. I wrote on the back, "I am the one who is living wave to wave, once again engaged in the dance."

My friend, Barb, created a vision board – a collage packed with words and pictures of all she wanted to attract in her life. Then, her mother died, and a few months later, Barb retired from three decades as a teacher, principal and teacher trainer. This habitually busy, highly organized woman, a member of several community service boards even while mentoring and evaluating student teachers, stepped away from her known life – a dual grief for her. She patiently sat with the unknowns of a future without regular work, allowing her grief to surface as it would. I encouraged her to trust her own wisdom to discern her new yeses.

Barb was amazed by how much spaciousness she quickly became

accustomed to. She knew she wanted to deepen her spiritual life and began to take unhurried time each morning to pray, reflect, journal and do a Virtues Pick. She decided to resign from all community Boards but one. She created a new vision board – this one reflecting a new simplicity, wordless beauty, clarity about the spare but ideal life she was ready to build. Shortly afterwards, she and her husband left for a trip to visit family in the Shetland Islands of North England and then went on to the south of France. I had never seen her happier or more at peace.

James, a member of my grief recovery group, simply found it impossible to stay in the house for long. The memories of his wife brought up too much pain. He created his own way of releasing it. He planned a long sailing trip with a couple of his adult children. Until departure, he worked on the boat, and got into shape by climbing trails through the mountains on our island.

Creativity is a powerful way to express and release our grief, and it brings amazing comfort. It's as if the nameless and shapeless cannot overwhelm one's soul completely. It gives us the strength to somehow contain it and renders it less oppressive. It also reveals what is calling to us from a new shore.

"The creative is the place where no one else has ever been. You have to leave the city of your comfort and go into the wilderness of your intuition. What you'll discover will be wonderful. What you'll discover is yourself."
Alan Alda, actor

SUSTAINING VIRTUES:

Creativity is the power of imagination. It is being open to inspiration, which ignites our originality. We dare to express our deepest feelings in new ways.

Openness is the willingness to consider new ideas. It is being receptive to the blessings and surprises of life.

HEALING STEPS:

1. Find the courage to express your experience of grief in your own creative way. Share it with others you trust. Place it somewhere you can view it or have access to it. It is a touchstone for honoring your deepest feelings.

2. In some creative way, whether in words or another form, record the journey of your new life as it unfolds.

41 A NEW SEASON

"To everything there is a season,
and a time to every purpose under heaven:
A time to be born, and a time to die...
A time to break down and a time to build up;
A time to weep and a time to laugh;
A time to mourn, and a time to dance..."
Ecclesiastes 3

In the days and months after a death, we may find ourselves buffeted by varying currents of emotion, from relief to gratitude to sorrow to anger. The space that the departed person occupied in our lives and our love is now vacant. Yet, it contains a fertile medium for new growth. We may not perceive it for a long while, but eventually, we will realize it. It is, whether welcome or not, an opportunity to start over.

As we are gradually adjusting to the first months and years without our loved one, we find ourselves at a fork in the road, a new decision point. The question arises, what season is this in my life?

Caterpillar Dreaming
The re-emergence of one's identity without the other who has gone is a slow process. We cannot rush it or push it. Rather, we need to summon unprecedented mercy for ourselves in order to breathe through the days, weeks and months when grief is so intrusive.

There is a long incubation period, when one's emotional skin is tissue thin and hypersensitive. It is a time of deep inner changes and shifts. It is helpful to know that this too shall pass, although when other people tell us that, it can feel like a slap of invalidation.

We need to honor this stage of life by cocooning as we are able, setting boundaries that give us the time and space for healing. If our lives are full of family or work responsibilities it would be wise to put on hold whatever tasks can be deferred, and instead take protected moments or hours to process this experience. This is the reason why getting away where one can breathe deeply and just be, is so helpful.

As I've said, the journey of grief has elements of Post-Traumatic Stress. Some of us even have a startle response when we hear a siren, or wake in the night sweating from nightmares. My sister-friend, Cheryll Simmons, one of the most literate, eloquent women I know, emailed me what I consider a perfect description of this phenomenon:

> *Healing... my mind is on healing. I picture trauma ripping and melting the myelin sheaths off nerves, the nerves that need this protection in order to insulate us from total vulnerability and the superlatives of everyday emotions: sadness becomes despair, worry becomes hopelessness, regret becomes self-blame, fear becomes panic and paranoia. Now those sheaths must grow back, so I can be in one place at a time, able to read my book – a statement instead of some syllables, a page instead of a paragraph – without the terrible black wings of disaster flapping in my face.*

A life-changing loss can turn us inside out. Not only a death, but when the last child leaves the home nest, when we retire, develop an illness, make a move, there is a vacancy of the familiar that sooner or later must be filled. A new homecoming beckons on the other side of the emptiness. We are called to reassess, review, and revise our life design. If we choose to make this a mindful process, it can lead us to fresh happiness.

As author Christina Baldwin says, "Change is the egg of the phoenix." Inherent in the human spirit is the impulse to rise from the ashes over and over. My widowed friend Jackie recently told me in a tearful phone call, "I need to move. This house is all about 'us'. I need to find my way to 'me'".

People promised me, in the midst of my bereavement, that I would eventually get to the other side. Thankfully, that has happened. I find that this cataclysmic change created a new opening in my life.

I became aware that like Alice, I could fall into a hole of sorrow and loss – or venture deeply into trust, taking the necessary time to discern what this season of my life would hold.

Shed Old Skin

Part of the process of opening to what we really want to do or be involves letting go of what no longer fits our lives. The death of someone close is a profound wake-up call, bringing a new perspective on what matters and what doesn't. I began to recognize a new strength which had grown while I was unaware of it – a sense that if I could get through losing John, I could handle anything. Once we face the loss of one who is such a central presence in our lives, other annoyances, demands, and frustrations are relegated to trivia. Talk about a values clarification!

First, there is the clearing of your loved one's belongings that needs to be done. This can be a healing time, releasing tears as you come across the memories. Marcel Proust said, "We think we no longer love our dead, but...suddenly we catch sight again of an old glove and burst into tears." I remember that happening to me when I caught sight of John's moccasin slippers. It triggered the memory of kneeling to help him get them on. It took me a while to be able to let them go.

If you find this task too daunting, get help with it. Others in the family or a friend may be more detached and can accelerate the process. Dan was an enormous help, bringing order and energy to the process of disposing of John's many belongings. On the streets of Victoria, men who shop at Good Will are walking around looking spiffy in John's jackets and jeans. Our brother Tommy who is a court interpreter happily took many of John's ties from his Disney executive days.

Give yourself the first choice of what to keep and then, family and friends. It will mean a lot to them to have something of the departed one's to treasure. Then let the rest go.

When you are ready, begin to do the same sifting process with your own possessions. Richard, a university professor who attended a Pace of Grace retreat with me and Dan, made a commitment to clean his home office which had been buried under piles of books and papers for decades. He could barely breathe in that room and he felt that his creativity was stymied as well. When he had completed the process, he said, "I crossed a new threshold in my known life." Our physical environment can block our joy and our clarity if it is cluttered with things we no longer use or need.

Be Willing to Transform

We may have no idea what we really want and that's natural. Hold the question lightly in gentle discernment. Avoid stuffing or numbing your feelings with alcohol or prescription drugs. Get through the grief bravely, and it will leave you clean and ready. As you release what you no longer need or want, clarity will begin to flow.

This is a time to deeply consider what really, truly matters to us and what doesn't. What habits are we ready to shed? One decision I made as I contemplated life without John was that I will no longer be driven by guilt of any kind. I will be accountable to my own sense of integrity, taking others' expectations or disappointments as possible teachable moments, including family dramas around what I "shoulda, coulda" done in the past. But I will not be dragged down into despair or take on their soul work as my own. I will use guilt only as a signal for change, not as a lifestyle or a signature perfume. For me, this meant keeping my sense of excellence while giving up perfectionism.

As we discern what we are ready to say "Yes" to, we also need to know our "No's". Not every opportunity can be taken. Because we can do something doesn't mean we should. This is a chance to seek what a young skate-boarder once described as "pristine momentum".

Seek Sustainable Balance

Life has a way of balancing everything. When there is injury, there is healing. When there is loss, there is gain. When the old has been released, the new must take its place. The healing process of grieving takes time, and it brings a new relationship to oneself and to everyone else in one's world. When we allow ourselves to be spiritually open, we find that in the space loss has carved out of us, new growth is beginning.

> *"What the caterpillar calls the end of the world,*
> *the master calls a butterfly."*
> Richard Bach, Author

SUSTAINING VIRTUES:

Purity is living in a state of physical and spiritual health. We experience wellbeing by keeping our bodies and living spaces clean and fresh. Purification is a process. We free ourselves day by day from unwanted influences and addictive desires. We let go of what no longer fits our lives. We replace negativity with virtues practices. We clean up our mistakes, choosing responsibility instead of guilt. Like a mirror kept free of dust, we purify our intentions. Purity gives us a clear conscience and a peaceful soul. Purity frees us to be who we are meant to be. It gives us a fresh start.

Simplicity is being content with the basic gifts of life. We live reflectively and mindfully, aware of what is important and what is not. We cherish those we love. We keep around us only what is useful or beautiful. We let go of excess, clutter and complexity. Simplicity gives us clarity and single-pointed concentration. It frees our minds from the stress of overdoing. We appreciate the little things, daily joys, and opportunities to be kind. We live in the moment and savor what is right before our eyes. We enjoy simply being.

HEALING STEPS:

1. As you find yourself emerging from the depths of grief and

riding the waves more gently, be kind to yourself and let guilt drift away with the grief. Your loved one would want you to be happy.

2. A helpful exercise is to reflect on and journal: What do I need to STOP doing, KEEP doing, and START doing to live with more grace and joy?

3. Maintain a consistent mindful awareness of what drains you or sustains a sense of grace in your life.

42 DISCERN YOUR YESES

"Tell me, what is it you plan to do
with your one wild and precious life?"
Mary Oliver, American poet

There are two reasons to give ourselves as much space as possible
after a death. First, healthy engagement in the grieving process
takes much of our energy. Secondly, as we gradually come back
to ourselves, the opening carved out by loss offers itself to us to
be refilled.

Set Your Inner House in Order

As you get back to the routines and responsibilities of life without
your loved one, take your sweet time to ask yourself what you
need at this new season of your life. Hold the question lightly, in a
trusting, contemplative way. The virtue of discernment will bring
you clarity. Although I found it took months before I could think
clearly about what I wanted in my life without John, I knew at a
deep level that this was a unique life-changing opportunity.

As our grief heals, it is as if we have shed an old skin, and a tender
new body is emerging. Habits or work we have been accustomed to
for years may no longer fit, or for some, familiar routines may be a
salvation in adjusting to a new normal.

Detach From Expectations

One of the things we need to give up at some time in life is the
guilt-oriented drive to meet the expectations or approval of others,
including our parents and our children! It now amazes me that I
was ever under the tyranny of anyone's sense of entitlement. It is
another door I will never willingly re-enter.

As we discern what we are ready to say "Yes" to, we also need to
know our "No's". Not every opportunity can be taken. Because we
can do something doesn't mean we should. This is a chance to seek
what a young skate-boarder once described as "pristine momentum".

One decision I made as I contemplated life without John was that I will no longer be driven by guilt of any kind. I will be accountable to my own sense of integrity, taking others' expectations or disappointments only as possible teachable moments, including family dramas around what I ``shoulda, coulda`` done in the past. But I will not be dragged down into despair or take on others' soul work as my own. I will use guilt only as a signal for change, not as a lifestyle or a signature perfume. For me, this meant keeping my sense of excellence while giving up perfectionism. I made this promise to myself in the second year after John's passing, when I kept hearing him whisper to me, "Be happy, Lin. Life is so short." Guilt comes from the ego and is closely related to fear – of not being loved, accepted, thought well of. When I feel the tug of that old feeling, I don my T-shirt that says, "I just realized…I don't care," and laugh my way through the day.

I had stepped away from my role as coordinator and chief communicator, along with Dan, of our global Virtues Project now in more than 98 countries, in order to care for John. I simply couldn't and wouldn't return. It loomed as an impossible burden I no longer had the heart to carry. I found that I needed a whole new way to spend my precious time. Others need to get back to their regular life as soon as possible. What matters most is that we take the time to ask ourselves the question, what do I really want now? What do I need?

The death of the youngest founder was a wake-up call that Dan and I would be shuffling off this mortal coil as well. It was time to pass the torch with a succession plan sooner rather than later. We took a drive through the Rocky Mountains and I held the question of what that would look like prayerfully. One day, Dan and I sat together, and he said, "Why don't we just expand the board?", which now consisted of just the two of us. I asked him, "Who would we appoint?" Four faithful individuals immediately came into my mind, and then Dan named them as well. Every one of them expressed honor at being asked, and a new circle of shared responsibility was formed.

Learning to ask for help, especially for an inveterate helper, is in itself a wonderful new freedom. And it spreads the generosity around. One shouldn't always hog it to oneself. It is egotistical to always want to be the giver.

Build Your Inner Circle

One of my yeses had to do with re-channelling the task-focused energy I had been spending for more than twenty years into my relationships. One of my top priorities these days is nurturing my own family and friendships as faithfully as I have nurtured the Virtues Community.

Just as I needed far more solitude and silence in the first year or two after John's passing, I also needed more regular contact with my closest friend since high school, Evelyn, who lives outside of Chicago. Instead of calling one another every month or so, we began a weekly check-in. We became more faithful story-keepers for one another.

I had become close friends with one of my colleagues on the Hospice board and we continued to nurture our friendship. My two sons showed a tenderness that drew us closer as well. And there were, and are, others whom I feel privileged to consider part of a mutual circle of love and support.

One of the greatest gifts of this time was a whole new relationship with my brother Tommy, John's twin, who lives in Puerto Rico. Having had a shallow relationship for years, we spanned a chasm of indifference with forgiveness and openness. We now have rendezvous in fun places, and are in regular contact. We adore each other, and admit we are the closest either of us can get to John.

Give Your Passion Permission

I thought that when I retired, someone would have to pry me away, leaving nail marks in my desk, yet here I was giving myself the freedom not to return to responsibility as I had known it. Dan and I did a lot of talking about the fact that we were ready to retire from the constant worldwide travel. The question was, what did we, individually and together, want to say yes to now? How could we do what we love and love what we do?

To my surprise, speaking and teaching in exotic locations no longer held the old allure. I referred many requests in Europe, the Caribbean, the Pacific and Asia to virtues facilitators. I am far more likely to say an enthusiastic yes to speaking at local conferences.

Writing was what truly ignited my passion. This book became my life's work. At the same time, a novel started populating itself in the back of my mind – my first.

I have a new, more leisurely pace of life, focusing on my health as never before. Dan has contentedly been restoring our home and property with the time he now has free of travel. He is healthier and slimmer. And he has undertaken several scholarly projects.

So, are you a gardener? A weaver? A sailor? A putterer? A writer? A reader? A volunteer? Say yes to what ignites your deepest enthusiasm.

"Don't ask yourself what the world needs. Ask yourself what makes you come alive, and go do that, because what the world needs is people who are alive."
Gil Bailie, Founder, the Cornerstone Forum

SUSTAINING VIRTUES:

Perceptiveness is clarity of insight. It is being observant of what is beneath the surface and looking for the deeper meaning. When we are perceptive, our understanding is intuitive and discerning. We slow down into awareness. We enter our observer mind to see what is truly real.

Devotion is commitment to something we care about deeply. It is wholehearted service to our life's purpose. What calls to us so strongly we cannot resist it, knowing it is truly ours to do?

HEALING STEPS:

1. Keep noticing the things that you love, the people you enjoy. Don't allow energy vampires to dominate your life; limit their impact with clear boundaries. Spend time doing and being what truly resonates with your soul.

2. Make a visual of what you are ready to attract and create in your life. A vision board, a soul collage, a sculpture, or a painting. Let it serve as your talisman.

3. Take action to make the life changes that call to you. Make a simple 90-day plan of three things you will do or change that will give you the joyful quality of life you are ready to claim. Put a favourite quote at the top and the dates for this three month period in the center.

4. Dedicate something you are doing to your loved one, whether an act of kindness, or a new creative project.

43 KEEP A PACE OF GRACE

"Lie quietly on the earth
that sky may send its strength through you
into the spinning planet."
Judith Billings, poet

As the intensity of grief mercifully fades, one of the legacies death brings in its wake is the awareness that our earthly life will not go on forever. I, for one, felt deep gratitude for this unexpected gift, a heightened sense of how precious and fleeting life is. As someone who has witnessed many deaths in my work at hospice, I would not have believed how much more this reality penetrated my awareness after John's death.

As we discern the changes required by our true yeses, one of the most important questions we need to ask ourselves is what pace do we want to keep now? For some, there is a need to pick up the pace, to add more adventure, to change one's choice of careers or primary activities. What is it that holds meaning for us now?

Others whose lives are full and whose normal pace involves constant multi-tasking, may long for a gentler rhythm, one that contains fewer obligations and responsibilities. When you are a primary caregiver to the dying, it can be all-consuming. It forces you to step away from everything else. Having tasted this freedom, you may never return.

Plant with Care
When planning a garden, enthusiasm can get us into trouble. We think, I'll plant some of these, and a bunch of these, and before we know it, the plot is far too overwhelming to take care of. When stepping back into new life, carefully select the size of your plot. What do you have the energy to tend that will also tend you? What colors, flavors, activities and people truly nurture you? If you can, let them in little by little. Keep assessing how much is enough. One day Dan and I were sitting together and I said to

him, "I'm really seeing that less is so much more." "And more is so much less," he replied, smiling.

Eliminate Excess

Give yourself full permission to sort out what you are ready for at any given time. Then, let people know. No one can abuse your time or your boundaries without your consent.

If something has kept you feeling stuck or thwarted, consider releasing or replacing it. If a job situation, a relationship, or the color of your living room walls has bored or oppressed you, be creative and find a way to change it. What virtue do you need to call on in recreating this part of your life? Is it moderation or passion? Forgiveness or justice?

Resist the tyranny of the telephone. Just because it rings doesn't mean it is compulsory to answer it. I have let people know that I have phone hours, which are typically two hours of the day when I'm willing to talk. Whether you work in an office or at home, people appreciate knowing when they are likely to reach you. I write in the mornings, so most people don't even try to call me then. I have a short period in early afternoon before I rest, and another just after dinner when I have attention to give to conversation, a walk with a friend, or a phone conference. After dinner, other than a short post-prandial burst of energy, I'm toast. My children know never to call me short of a life or death emergency after 7 PM. They probably think of it as the witching hour.

Most people, even my closest friends, know that if they want to speak to me for any length of time on the phone, they email for an appointment. It works well for them too, to know when we will be talking. These boundaries may not work for people who enjoy the immersion in social media, from Facebook to twitter and whatever is current now. For me, they are an intrusion, perhaps because I have had so many people and audiences in my life.

Emails and calls can consume so much of our energy that they easily distract from the single-pointed concentration that allows us to focus on what is most important to us.

Honor Your Spirit

My friend Barb and her husband took their 14 year-old grand-daughter Larissa to Hawaii. One morning, Barb was typing away at emails, and Larissa said, "Nan, what are you doing?" She then told Barb that she had decided not to do emails and to shut off her cell phone, making just one call to her mother to let her know they had arrived safely. She plunged into the welcoming sea, snorkeling for hours. One afternoon, Barb saw her swimming strangely with arms outstretched for a long way down the beach and out toward the reef. Then she turned and quickly swam back to shore. Larissa came running up, shaking. She said, "I`m really scared and really excited. I was snorkeling along and suddenly a huge turtle came up under one of my hands, then another one under my other hand. They took me out to the reef." What a sacred experience. In contrast, I have witnessed young women totally distracted by their cell phones from being present to magnificent vistas on a lake excursion in the Rockies. The choice Larissa made honored her own spirit and opened her to wonder.

Being receptive to the virtue of wonder when we have gone through a huge change like a death is a chance for deep rebalancing. There is no right or wrong here, just a clear awareness of what stresses you and what blesses you.

Put Your First Passion First

My sister friend, Jill, an artist John, Dan and I have loved for decades, had an experience in meditation one night that she shared with me. It came to her to practice the Law of Fives. In her full, busy life this involved five 3-hour periods each day:

First for shower, breakfast, walking, reflection.
Second for painting.
Third for lunch, rest, household errands or work.
Fourth, for dinner, family time at the table, emails and calls.
Fifth, more painting before bed.

This is a woman who, when she began painting, could disappear into it for fifteen hours a day. Jill knew that this new concept would give her a more sustainable life.

As a general principle, set aside your most energized hours for whatever is most important to you and keep that time sacrosanct. Before breakfast, I exercise with yoga or a walk, then eat breakfast, do my RPMS – reflection, prayer meditation, journaling and Virtues Pick. Then, I`m ready to write. I don't allow anything to disturb me. I don't even check emails until I have had my morning writing time. No one has ever died by not hearing from me instantly. As Dan says, there are no virtues emergencies. If I do choose to answer the phone the odd time, I set a time to call back when I am ready to talk. To me, this is not selfish; it's self-preservation. And it is good modeling for others. It tells the world we are not at the mercy of their expectations.

Rest Proactively
Grief is exhausting. Get into the habit of resting before you get tired and then keep it up! Rest allows us to be at our best, and our most productive. Whether leaning back in your car during a lunch hour or taking a good book and lying on the couch, take at least twenty minutes about six hours after you awaken to rest your body and your mind. The purpose of reading an engaging novel is that it prevents "monkey mind" when your mind keeps running in circles and refuses to shut off.

Take Time to Play
I love the cartoon that shows two elders sitting together and one says, "What do you want on your tombstone?" The other says, "Got it all done. Died anyway."

As often as you can, every day if possible, do something fun that isn't on your task list. My new addiction of choice, which takes me out of my head and gives me relief from emotions as well, is jig saw puzzles. I like crossword puzzles as well, and both are good for aging brains.

Many of my friends love to play in their gardens. It restores their souls. Meet friends for a meal. Try new recipes. Build something with those tools that have been sitting in the garage. Dan's work of deconstructing and rebuilding the decks surrounding our home took him two years after John's passing. "I'm slow but relentless" he would say. As he was designing the custom flower boxes for our spring flowers, he would sit in a rocker, puffing on his pipe, quietly contemplating the design before he began. I believe it gave him a creative outlet while keeping him in shape and also giving me the brand new deck I wanted.

Pace yourself. Find your own balance for work, play, and rest, one that gives you the fullest sense of contentment.

> *"Moderation is the silken string running through the pearl chain of all virtues."*
> Joseph Hall, English Bishop & author

SUSTAINING VIRTUES:

Moderation is being content with enough. We call on self-discipline to create balance in our lives, to keep from overdoing. We are healthy stewards of our time and resources.

Contentment is the awareness of sufficiency, a sense that we have enough and we are enough. We appreciate the simple gifts of life.

HEALING STEPS:

1. Take your time to decide how you wish to manage your time. You are the author of your own life.

2. Balance work, play, rest and recreation, including a routine of reverence. Be creative in choosing the best structure for your days.

3. Be assertive about who, when, and how you will communicate. It's really your call!

44 GRACE VISITS

"Those who have passed on through death, have a sphere of their own. It is not removed from ours…there is no real separation…In prayer there is a mingling of stations, a mingling of condition. Pray for them as they pray for you! When you do not know it, and are in a receptive attitude, they are able to make suggestions to you, if you are in difficulty."
'Abdu'l-Baha, Baha'i Writings

One of the great mysteries is whether or not we can communicate with those who have died. My belief is that in death souls cross over into a spiritual realm. They live, work and create in that world, and they are able to help those of us still in the physical world. They are still here, but in a different dimension.

Friends often ask me if I have had any visits from John's spirit. Several times, I have, in one form or another, and always unexpectedly. I have spoken with many others who have experienced moments of connection when they felt the presence of one they love who has died. A vision, a voice, a dream, a sudden synchronicity, or a song, are portals through which, I believe, angels dare to tread. It doesn't happen to everyone who is bereaved, but having a regular spiritual practice of deep listening may well help us to connect in this way.

Dreams of You
One night, at a time when the first waves of bereavement began to sweep me off my feet, I had a clear dream of John. I was standing at the front desk of a hotel, and he walked up beside me. When I turned to look at him, he was wearing a long-sleeved, forest green shirt, and beige pants. He was his normally slim self, and looked about thirty-five. He was very energized and cheerful and looked at me with a big smile. In the dream I fainted. When I journaled that morning during my prayer time, I asked John what his message was. Instantly his voice came into my mind saying, "Lin, I'm right beside you, in a parallel world, in the one world of God." I asked what it meant that I had fainted. "You are faint-hearted right now."

To be honest, I found this dream less comforting than annoying, as if John was saying that since he hadn't really left, why was I so sad? I wasn't ready to be done with my grief, and was quite put off by his timing. I was faint hearted. I didn't care about the spiritual teachings I had believed in all my life. I had lost him and I wasn't ready to be reconciled to that! Later, of course, I appreciated the gesture.

People I have companioned about the death of a loved one have told me many times of dreams in which the individual came to them to say goodbye, to tell them they were happy and well, or to answer their questions.

Call on Your A-Team
The week after John died, I did feel the comfort of his presence, when I was sitting at our dining room table with a legal sized yellow lined pad in front of me, with a four-page list of things to arrange as Executor to settle John's affairs. I had met with our lawyer and was amazed by all there was to do. I felt utterly overwhelmed and exhausted just looking at it. "How can I possibly do this?" I wondered silently, "even with Dan's help?" Suddenly, I heard John say very firmly, "Lin, remember your Vitamin T (Trust). You were my blue angel. Now I'll be yours." A deep sense of peace filled me, and I got to work on the list. Three days later, to the astonishment of our lawyer, Dan and I had everything on the list either done or in process.

I have often written and spoken about my belief based on many years of research into the world's sacred texts, as well as my own personal experiences with the dying, that each of us has what I call an "A-Team", consisting of ancestors, angels, and advisors. If we fail to call on them, or remain open to the inner promptings they send us, we lose the connection, although it is always there waiting for us to enter a state of trust and openness. To me, if we don't ask for their help, we're promoting unemployment after death! It is their mission to assist us. To me, they are the voice, the hands, the help sent by God when we need them.

Our ancestors are generations of family members who have gone before us. Advisors are those who have the expertise to help us with anything, including saints such as St. Anthony who can help us find lost articles or even lost thoughts. Angels, according to some sacred traditions, from Catholicism to the Baha'i Faith, are direct emanations of God, like rays of the sun. They include the angels of virtues such as the Angel of Peace, the Angel of Truth, the Angel of Joy, the Angel of Justice. One of the ways I like to pray for others, particularly my children, is to ask one or more of these angels to hold, protect, and help them.

One of the times John came to me suddenly and unbidden was just a few days after he died, when his two long awaited retirement checks arrived, and I went to the bank to put them into his estate account. They were essential in order to continue paying the mortgage on his house, taxes, and other expenses. I was shaky that day, having just buried John, but determined to get some things done for him. A business-like woman ushered me into her office. I had met her once before and she had worked with John before. I sat down across the desk, expecting her to say something, if only a simple, "I'm sorry for your loss." She just started typing away on her computer, not saying a word of welcome or condolence. I swallowed down my disappointment and just put the two checks on her desk, saying, "I want to deposit these into John's estate account." "Oh, you can't do that," she said, "They're not made out to 'the estate of.'" They were from the U.S. Treasury and Social Security Administration. "You'll have to send them back and get them reissued." "What? But they are his money and need to go into his estate to pay his bills. We don't have the money for that!" "Well," she said, lips pressed firmly, "I've been here thirty years and I can tell you it isn't possible." I nearly burst into tears. "That's ridiculous," I said. "It's his money. They are made out to him. And if I send them back, we will probably never see them again." She kept reiterating her thirty years. Finally, I yelled, "You know I've just lost my brother. You could at least be kind!" She paled visibly. Suddenly I felt John beside me with his hand on my shoulder and my Dad on the other side, as if they were gently pulling me back. John whispered, "Vitamin T, Linda! Vitamin T."

The thought came to my mind that God has the power to take care of anything. I sat back, took a deep breath, and smiled at her, at which she became even paler. What came out of my mouth surprised me as much as it did her. "I'd appreciate it if you would call your legal department and check." She started babbling about thirty years again, and I repeated once only, "Please call your legal department." She did, and was put on hold for at least ten minutes. I chatted with her amiably and found out that after hours she was a dog trainer. Later, I told Dan "Maybe that's why she treats people like dogs." I'm not proud of it, but it felt good to say it at the time.

When the lawyer finally came on the line, the banker called her the unlikely name of Clarabelle. I immediately thought of the Howdy Doody clown John, Tommy and I had loved as children. The banker said, "What??!!! But I've been here thirty years and we've never..." Clarabelle shut her up quickly. She got off the phone and in icy tones said, "Yes, apparently you can deposit the checks." I barely resisted shouting "Na ner nah nah!" at her. Just thanked her and left. And then I thanked John.

It's All in the Timing
When we had the huge estate sale at John's home to sell many of his household belongings, I found it very daunting. Dan had agreed to conduct the sale but was ill that day, and I had to go alone. As I drove up the hill to John's home, I felt very anxious. I didn't like this sort of thing to begin with but how would I feel letting go of his things? Suddenly, I heard his voice in my mind saying, "Lin, we are here to help you. You're not alone." I wondered if that was my own wishful thinking or had John really spoken to me? I turned on the radio and the announcer said, "...here to help you." – a small but significant confirmation. The sale went seamlessly without any of the usual garage sale haggling. I had a sign on the wall saying most of the proceeds would be donated to earthquake relief in Haiti. Amazingly, no one argued with the sticker price and one young man gave more, "for a good cause" he said. Later that week we sent

EPILOGUE: JOY IN THE MOURNING

*"She was no longer wrestling with the grief,
but could sit down with it as a lasting companion
and make it a sharer in her thoughts."*
George Eliot, English novelist

My father, Borrah Kavelin, used to speak about joy and sorrow embracing, clasping his hands and interlacing his fingers. I never truly understood what it meant until the second year after John's death, when the storms of grief were no longer raging and had gentled into occasional ripples of sadness. It felt more as if John was just away on a long trip. Dan would say, "At this age, we'll see him any minute."

For me, the sorrow never departed entirely, but a fresh sense of joy began to flow, like a new current through my awareness. The tides of grief had somehow excavated a new depth of awareness of the exquisite fragility of this treasured life. My grief counsellor, Tom, was right. I was better. More focused, clearer about what I wanted at this time in my life, more dedicated to sustaining my pace of grace than ever before, not only as a rhythm of life but as a response to the presence of God's abiding Grace.

As I've said, some bereaved individuals feel guilty for their surreptitious joy in being alive, as if it is a betrayal of their love and loyalty to the one who has died. But it is nothing of the kind. Our happiness is a gift to the departed. Perhaps it allows them to move on with greater peace.

The Gratitude Antidote
As a practitioner of virtues for decades, one of the great gifts which I have received is the wisdom of consciously choosing gratitude as a balm for anxiety and sadness.

One day, during my morning reflection time, I sat in my prayer corner, gazing out at the Pacific through my east facing window. I was feeling very anxious about the waiting priorities that demanded to be completed. I was still feeling drained by surges of grief, but life went on and I had commitments to keep. I went outside onto the deck in the fresh spring air. I asked what virtue I needed and gratitude swiftly came to mind. So I began counting my blessings. The sweet scent of sun-infused pine boughs, the beauty of mountains, sea and forest in our island paradise on the west coast of British Columbia, the love of my husband, my faith, my children, my friends, the creativity of being a writer, the completion of most of my role as John's executor. As the list went on and on, I felt a smile melting away my tension, and my breathing changed. I felt happy, at peace, ready for the day.

Gratitude is one virtue we can never have too much of. It is a healing remedy for lingering regret, sadness, and anxiety. It ushers in its sister virtues of peace, contentment and serenity.

Affirm Your Life
Affirmations are a helpful tool in the process of grief recovery. Keep them in the present tense rather than the future "I do" instead of "I will."

Some that I have found meaningful are:
"I love my easy, grace-filled life."
"I am grateful for my rich, full, life."
"I live fully and joyfully."
"Every day is a good day."

Seek Serene Efficiency
I have often sensed John's presence, encouraging me to be happy. I feel he wants me to live mindfully, and to protect my newborn joy, living each moment to the fullest.

There is something about the certainty of death that is a huge relief. None of us is indispensable. As John's physical and mental capacities waned, I watched his uber-responsible attitude fade and a new radiant serenity take its place. He taught me so much about how to move from doing to being. He showed me how to be the calm in the winds of tests, to trust whatever comes to pass.

More than ever before in my life, having navigated the journey of extreme grief, I found I was able to suffuse serenity into the tasks of each day. Knowing what matters and what doesn't puts everything into proper perspective. Looming pressures lose their power.

Steve Jobs said something profound as he consciously faced his own death:
> "Remembering that I'll be dead soon is the most important tool I've ever encountered to help me make the big choices in life. Because almost everything – all external expectations, all pride, all fear of embarrassment or failure – these things just fall away in the face of death, leaving only what is truly important. Remembering that you are going to die is the best way I know to avoid the trap of thinking you have something to lose. You are already naked. There is no reason not to follow your heart."

Be a Faithful Friend to Yourself
If I were to describe the essence of Graceful Endings, it would be that the most healing way to navigate the experience of loss and grief is to befriend our grief throughout the journey, trusting its ebb and flow. Knowing we have the strength to go the distance, we allow ourselves to relish the deepening sense of aliveness that can come in its wake. Surrounding ourselves with people who love us and are able to companion us gives us the safety net that catches us when we start to go under.

I am completing Graceful Endings in Aitutaki, Cook Islands – the same beautiful island where I started my book, A Pace of Grace, eight years ago. It feels as though I have come full circle.

May you find that this journey brings you to a place of joy, in which you can choose how to fill the hours and God willing, the years left to you in this world, in ways that fulfill your truest dreams.

As grief wends its way through our lives, we have the choice to open more and more to the joys of a new life. Yes, we are changed forever by loss. We can learn to view these changes as grist for God's mill, creating new spiritual capacity, not only to survive but to live more deeply, opening to the grace each day brings.

Linda Kavelin-Popov
Aitutaki, Cook Islands

APPENDIX A: RESOURCES

WEBSITES

www.gracefulendings.net for Linda's blog, Johns last lectures, photos, talks by Linda, and more

www.virtuesproject.com for information and many free downloads from The Virtues Project as well as how to order Virtues Reflection Cards and other resources

www.paceofgrace.net for information on Linda's book, *A Pace of Grace.*

www.emedicinehealth.com/end-of-life_decision_making/article_em.htm

For more on *The Five Wishes* document by Jim Towey, recognized in most states in the US and can be used along with signing documents required in one's own area. It is available on line at **www.agingwithdignity.org/forms/5wishes.pdf**

www.nlm.nih.gov/medlineplus/hospicecare.html for general information on hospice care

www.abta.org American Brain Tumor Association

www.mattieonline.com for information on Mattie Stepanek

www.animas.org for information on Bill Plotkin's *Soulcraft* and stages of life

www.caringbridge.org A free service that makes it easy to update friends and family worldwide when a loved one is ill or dying.

http://defoore.com/ArticleHealthyGrievingTechniques.htm

www.elderthink.com/memory for much valuable information on grief

www.jalaliyyihquinn.com and jalaljalalart@gmail.com
for the art of Jalaliyyih Quinn, whose painting is on the cover

http://www.menweb.org/mangrief.htm on men and grief

http://www.videocaregiving.org/ a visual education center for
caregivers

www.soulcollage.com for information on how to do Soul Collage
Find the Hospice website in your region.

BOOKS

Susanne Alexander's *Empowered Healing*: Creating Quality of Life
while Journeying with Cancer

Maggie Callanan and Patricia Kelley's *Final Gifts*

Steven Levine's *Unattended Sorrow; Who Dies?* and his other books
on death and dying.

Bill Plotkin's *Soulcraft*: Crossing into the Mysteries of Nature and
Psyche

Linda Kavelin-Popov's *A Pace of Grace* for modalities of meditation
and 10 Rules for Health.

Joan Didion's *Year of Magical Thinking*

APPENDIX B: GLOSSARY

ACT with Tact Positivity Sandwich: This is a virtues based way to give feedback tactfully. A: Appreciate, giving someone a virtue you notice in them, C: Correct: respectfully ask for a positive change in the way they speak or act, and T: Thank them for a virtue that you appreciate. This allows them to hear your perspective in a way that doesn't create defensiveness and allows them to be open to what you are saying.

Advance Directive: also known as living will, personal directive, advance directive, or advance decision, is a set of written instructions that a person gives that specify what actions should be taken for their health if they are no longer able to make decisions due to illness or incapacity. The instruction appoints someone, usually called an agent, to make such decisions on their behalf. A living will is one form of advance directive, leaving instructions for treatment. Another form authorizes a specific type of power of attorney or health care proxy, where someone is appointed by the individual to make decisions on their behalf when they are incapacitated. People may also have a combination of both. People are often encouraged to complete both documents to provide comprehensive guidance regarding their care. One example of a combination document is the *Five Wishes* advance directive in the United States. From Wikipedia

Anticipatory Grief: the grief that comes before death, when the dying and those who care for them begin to grieve the loss that is coming.

Breakthrough pain: when pain breaks through or penetrates despite efforts to medicate, without success.

Bereavement: grief that occurs after a death.

Cheyne-Stokes breathing: breathing with rhythmic waxing and waning of depth of breaths and regularly recurring apneic periods, when breath is suspended for several seconds.

DNR: In medicine, a "do not resuscitate" or "DNR", sometimes called a "No Code", is a legal order written either in the hospital or on a legal form to respect the wishes of a patient to not undergo CPR or advanced cardiac life support (ACLS) if their heart were to stop or they were to stop breathing. The DNR request is usually made by the patient or health care power of attorney and allows the medical teams taking care of them to respect their wishes. In the health care community "allow natural death" or "AND" is a term that is quickly gaining favor as it focuses on what is being done, not what is being avoided. A DNR does not affect any treatment other than that which would require intubation or CPR. Patients who are DNR can continue to get chemotherapy, antibiotics, dialysis, pain medication, or any other appropriate treatments.

Hospice: Hospice care is end of life care provided by health professionals and volunteers. They give medical, psychological and spiritual support. The goal of the care is to help people who are dying have peace, comfort and dignity. The caregivers try to control pain and other symptoms so a person can remain as alert and comfortable as possible. Hospice programs also provide services to support a patient's family.

Hyper-vigilance: is when a family member or caregiver becomes constantly tense and on guard, sharply alert, and often unable to sleep, with intense focus on the dying person, usually becoming more intense as death approaches.

Life Review: the common need dying persons have to look back at their lives, talk about successes, regrets, and memories of their lives. Companioning them without judgment or rationalization, just respectful, engaged curiosity is a great gift.

Living Will: This is another term for an advance directive about how a dying person wishes to be treated when he or she is no longer able to make decisions.

Medical Representation: This is a special kind of power of attorney, a legal form in which a trusted agent is appointed to make decisions when a dying person is no longer able to, usually a family member such as the primary caregiver.

Power of Attorney: a general assignment of authority to a trusted individual over a dying person's legal and financial affairs. This is a legal form which typically requires witnessing by a lawyer.

Probate: the first step in the legal process of administering the estate of a deceased person, resolving all claims and distributing the deceased person's property under a will. It typically takes months to a year to complete, and is necessary before all disbursements of a deceased person's estate can be made by the executor according to their will.

Sacred Texts: the Holy Books of the world's religions, such as the *Torah* of Judaism, the *Bible* of Christianity, the *Bhagavad-Gita* of Hinduism, the *Dhammapada* of Buddhism, the *Qu'ran* of Islam, the *Baha'i Writings* of the Baha'i Faith.

Made in the USA
Charleston, SC
08 October 2012